God's

Healing

Hope:

Breaking the Strongholds of Wrong Thinking

By John Livingston Clark

Order this book online at www.trafford.com/08-0199
or email orders@trafford.com

Most Trafford titles are also available at major online book retailers.

Edited by: Gail Huibregtse
Cover Design by: Eric Wester

Printed in Victoria, BC, Canada.

ISBN: 978-1-4251-7121-6 (sc)

Our mission is to efficiently provide the world's finest, most comprehensive book publishing service, enabling every author to experience success. To find out how to publish your book, your way, and have it available worldwide, visit us online at www.trafford.com/10510

www.trafford.com

North America & international
toll-free: 1 888 232 4444 (USA & Canada)
phone: 250 383 6864 • fax: 812 355 4082

Dedication

This book is dedicated to my loving parents, Buford and Elizabeth Clark, formerly of San Diego, California, but who now reside in the Dallas, Texas area.

Because of them I accepted Christ as my Savior at an early age.

Because of them I grew up learning moral values.

Because of them I learned to love music.

Because of them I developed pride in working hard.

Because of them I was encouraged to pursue teaching.

Because of them I was challenged to follow God throughout my life.

Thank you, Mom and Dad, for all that you have done for me.

Acknowledgements

I would like to extend my sincere thanks to the following people, all of whom have read my entire manuscript, or sections of it, and have given valuable constructive criticism. These people have spent countless hours evaluating this book to help make it the very best it can be to the glory of God, and to most effectively minister to the needs and hurts of the readers.

Sharon (Carlson) Graham-Laraene: M.S.W. (Master of Social Work), B.S.A. (Bachelor of Social Anthropology), and REV. (Ordained minister of the United Methodist Church). She is a professional, Christian counselor, formerly the executive director of Christian Counseling Services of Sunnyside, Washington. She is a former pastor of a church in Spokane, Washington. I received counseling from her for over 6 years. God used her to help transform my life, and as a result, to write this book.

Kate Braden Green: M.S., a certified high school counselor. Kate gave an extensive amount of evaluation that resulted in a lot of improvement to the manuscript and made it more relevant to the reader.

Sarah Friedrich, Associate Pastor in Christian Education, at Zillah Nazarene Church in Zillah, Washington.

Buford and Betty Clark, my beloved parents, to whom this book is dedicated.

Mike Beaver, John Newport, Dean Effler, and Jeff Deardorff, close personal friends and mentors.

Eric (Wes) Wester, and Melissa Wester, published authors, who gave insight and advice about the entire publishing process. These two people have written and illustrated a children's book entitled, "Playmation Time Machine." This book is available through Trafford Publishing. Eric is a very talented artist, who designed my cover.

Gail Huibregtse, my editor and proof reader, who is a high school journalism instructor, and long time friend. As a first time author, I could not have produced this book without her assistance.

My three sisters, Carol Cocking, Sylvia Faust, and Marcia Kawamoto, who all read the book from the perspective of growing up with me.

Thank you to Eric Stillwell, pastor of the Zillah Nazarene Church, who read the entire final manuscript.

Thank you to my wife and son, both of whom have helped me learn so much about myself.

I am grateful to all my wonderful prayer support partners.

I certainly cannot forget all of the other wonderful people at Trafford Publishing in Victoria, Canada, for putting together the final product, and Minuteman Press in Yakima, Washington, for assisting with the completion of the cover.

Table of Contents

Introduction

Every life has a story. This is mine. I am not a famous athlete, or a movie star. I am not a head-liner musician. What I am is seen only on Sunday morning, when people sit in church. I am the music worship leader, but the people didn't see the real me. I was a confused, frustrated, angry and depressed person with low self-esteem, a negative and defeated attitude, and a victim-failure mindset. I was in financial bondage. I carried this emotional baggage with me into my fifties. I lugged it around while I was in paid music ministry in local churches.

I thought, since I was Christian, I was not supposed to have all of these problems. It put me on a big guilt trip, it made me feel like a hypocrite, and I began to doubt my salvation. I came to the conclusion that either I was not a Christian at all, or there was something seriously wrong with my belief system as it concerned practical, day-to-day living. I continued experiencing the same struggles, habits, and problems with no positive change. I sang "Victory In Jesus," but had no victory. This led me to accept, subconsciously, a life of defeat. Looking back on it, I believe the music ministry became a vehicle to satisfy my low self-esteem by getting applauded and recognized for directing choirs and performing. I wore a big mask!

I had emotional issues from my past. This emotional garbage from as far back as childhood, weighed me down, but I didn't tell anyone. I wasn't even being honest with myself. Like millions of Christians, I was raised in a Christian home with a particular set of beliefs and values that was to be accepted, not challenged. My false belief system, combined with some experiences, hurt me more than helped me, and I am to some degree still paying the consequences.

In this book you will read about what these teachings and experiences were, and how they became a negative stronghold in my life. You will read about what I have had to do to start a recovery process, reprogram my thinking, and how I am different today.

You may be thinking, "Why should I care about this guy's story? How is it relevant to me?"

Answer. I believe it is representative of the experiences of many Christians.

This is a book on recovery, written primarily to Christians. People tend to think of recovery in terms of alcohol, drugs, pornography, smoking, or divorce. However, it can also include anger, codependency, depression, abuse, gambling, abandonment, eating disorders, spending/debt problems, low self-esteem, negativity, and relational problems.

Let's get a little bit more specific. There are things sometimes not thought of as being problems. Are you, as a professing Christian, experiencing any of the following? I have experienced most of these—

1. Bitterness or an unforgiving Spirit.
2. Jealousy.
3. Having a dominant attitude over someone.
4. You feel like you just can't help doing something.
5. You blame others when things are not right.
6. You take frustrations out on your spouse.
7. You withdraw from others.
8. You sometimes think other people have an ulterior motive.
9. You feel trapped in a situation.
10. You are afraid you will lose friendships, so you rescue people.
11. You have frequent feelings of unworthiness or discouragement.
12. You escape reality through fantasies or entertainment.

Many Christians have one or more of these sometimes "hidden" problems, and one of them could be the person sitting next to you on Sunday morning. Many people who attend church and other religious activities, have problems in their lives that they believe Christians should not have, and over which they are not experiencing victory. For various reasons of which they may not even be aware, they are being hindered from maturing as a Christian, and from moving ahead in life. These same believers may be bogged down in defeat and despair. They may be struggling with their identity as a Christian, and with life itself. They may feel trapped or "stuck" in a particular circumstance or mindset, with no way out. This paragraph described my life, and possibly describes yours also.

For many years I thought about writing a book, but believed I was held back because of low self-esteem. I have been challenged through many of the books I have read to enlarge my vision, dream God-sized dreams, and step out on faith to accomplish great things for Him. My greatest hurt can become my greatest ministry. Writing has been an emotional outlet for me. It has made it possible for me to rise above my circumstances and make the most of my resources and myself. Through the Holy Spirit's direction, I am making use of my abilities and following my dream. All that I need to write is a pen and a pad of paper. At the same time, I can make a difference in the lives of others. By sharing my story, I can get out of myself and focus on others, which is part of recovery.

What is said in the following pages can apply to anyone, whatever your religion, race, culture, or age. It is for anyone who sees the need to come out of their facades, face reality, and start living in hope and freedom, as God intended.

Chapter 1

AS A MAN THINKS, SO IS HE

One begins to practice their faith when they identify the thoughts that are keeping them from doing so.

I was born in Bellingham, Washington, but was raised in beautiful, sunny southern California. Being brought up in that part of the country has made me the envy of many people. Probably what I remember most about San Diego is taking walks on sandy beaches and watching the glimmering sunset reflecting off the ocean.

I have two wonderful parents who taught me honesty, responsibility, morality, and the value of hard work, among many other admirable qualities. My dad spent time with me. He taught me a lot about how to safely use tools. I learned how to paint and build things. One time we built an HO model train layout. I grew up at the beginning of the commercial jet age, when the Boeing 707 was a newcomer in the sky. My dad and I would often go down to Lindberg Field. He parked the car at a spot where those big jets would come right over the top of the car. My dad was supportive of my interests.

I have four wonderful sisters. Three of them, along with their families, live in Texas, Michigan, and California. The fourth one was stillborn, and has lived with Jesus in heaven ever since. The biggest tribute to my parents is that all of us are serving Jesus Christ.

My mom and dad have a very large spiritual family. Dad was a Baptist minister. That makes all of us PK's — preachers' kids. I am not going to speak for my sisters, but for me that meant "picked on kid." I have often asked myself the question, "Would any of us be Christians today if it were not for our parents?" Speaking for myself, I really don't know, but I am so glad I am and do not know what I would do if I weren't.

I accepted Jesus Christ as my savior at age ten. Let me explain because that means different things to different people. I believe that Christ is God in human flesh. I believe that He died on a cross and rose from the dead for me. Because of this, eternal life is possible, and it is not based on my works, but on His grace.

It was during vacation Bible school that I was baptized. Baptists believe in baptism by immersion. I not only got immersed, but I took in water. I did a rather dumb thing and opened my mouth under water. Up I came sputtering and gasping for air. All of the kids thought it was funny and started laughing at me.

The other thing I remember about my early church years was that a Sunday school teacher taught me that the word "JOY" stood for Jesus first, Others second, and Yourself fast. She meant well, in teaching me and the rest of the class to think more of others than ourselves, but at that young age, it started making me think too little of myself. I believe it was one of the first influences contributing to my low self-esteem.

Several school experiences come to mind. I started wearing glasses in grade school, and some of the kids called me "four eyes." I remember getting into a fight in fifth grade. I was the last chosen for sports. (Does that sound familiar to some of you?) In the locker room in junior high school, I vividly recall kids making fun of my body, especially my private parts. That was when all students were required to take showers. Again, these experiences were all whittling away at my self-esteem.

There were some positive experiences. I got an award for excellent penmanship in grade school, sold a lot of tickets door-to-door to the Boy Scout Fair, and had rapid success when I began playing the trumpet in the fifth grade. The negative experiences, unfortunately, had more influence on me than the positive.

Another thing I believe contributed to my low self-esteem was that I didn't know how to swim. My mom and dad told me that I knew how to swim when I was really young, but sometime after that a huge wave clobbered me, and I instantly became afraid of the water. Instead of being determined to learn to swim, I allowed myself to be dominated by that fear, even into my adult life. When most of the other kids at church camp could swim and jump off the diving board, I could be found at the shallow end of the pool. That also retarded my interaction with my peers and made me think less of myself. Because of not knowing how to swim, I also never made a high rank in Boy Scouts. As it turned out, a few years later I became a "girl scout." (I know, that is a really bad joke.)

As I look back on these experiences, a pattern was already developing. Instead of doing whatever it took to get ahead, I allowed myself to be held back by my own limitations and fears.

Music and playing the trumpet was something I was getting really good at. I got to be the bugler at Boy Scout camp one year. That meant that I got up earlier than everyone else, took my bugle out in the cold, walked to the lodge, and played *Reveille* over the PA system, which was piped into all of the cabins.

It sometimes is very difficult to play a brass instrument in the cold morning air with little or no warm-up. Most mornings I would miss a few notes. One morning I played it almost perfectly, and when I got done I remarked to the scout director that, "I did pretty good this time." To this he replied, "The microphone is still on." I heard about that when I got back to my cabin.

Music was a big part of my church experience. I played solos and helped accompany the hymns with my trumpet teacher and two violinists. I really enjoyed this part of church. Other than that, all through high school Christianity was no more than going to religious activities, believing the way I was supposed to believe, and adhering to certain "do's and don'ts" Sometimes I was the only person my age in church. There was very little relevancy to my daily life.

Up to this point, my school and church experiences were more negative than positive, except for music. When my family first moved to San Diego, my dad took a church in the Logan Heights area, which was an interracial community, and I had a lot of problems. I was definitely a "white boy." All that I have talked about up until now took place in a predominately Afro-American setting.

My high school years were fairly positive, even though I was still a minority. I wasn't involved in sports and didn't like to take physical education because of having to undress and take showers, a carry over from junior high school. When I had the opportunity to enlist in the California Cadet Corps (similar to R.O.T.C.), in place of physical education, I signed up. I had a lot of fun learning how to march and shoot rifles.

Of course, I was involved in the concert and marching bands. This was the year 1964. Skateboards were a hot, new commodity. As I soon would discover, marching bands and skateboards were not a good combination. A friend and I were going down a hill a few blocks from my house, when our skateboards locked together. Our boards stopped. We didn't! I sustained a knee injury. It was during marching season when the band was practicing half-time shows for football games, and I was the lead trumpet player. The band director, needless to say, was not very happy that I could not march for awhile.

I was somewhat reserved when it came to making friends, but I did have several people with whom I was close. One girl, in particular, a cute Caucasian, I tried to get as close to as possible, literally. It was my first dating experience.

Now, talk about change. In the middle of my junior year, my dad became the pastor of a church in a posh, beach community across the San Diego Bay, known as Coronado. This is primarily a Navy town, adjacent to North Island Naval Air Station. I was no longer called "white boy." Anyone who has lived in San Diego knows that this would be a radical adjustment, but a nice one. I mean, I wasn't complaining, especially when the family lived within walking distance of the beach.

I had mostly positive experiences in Coronado, but mainly because of music. There I played in not only the marching band, but also in the jazz band. This was where I developed a love for playing jazz.

I had two close friends. One was a Navy brat, who was also a trombone player in the band. He was able to get me on the Navy base, where we went to see movies and play pool for dirt cheap prices. The other friend I had was a Presbyterian minister's son. We, of course, had a lot in common, since we were both preachers' kids.

One other thing I need to mention about high school is that I started to recognize that I had ability to write. I seemed to have a natural "knack" for writing and always received good grades on my papers. The same trend would continue through college. As I look back on this now, I am thinking that maybe I should have given some serious consideration, at the time, to going into the writing field.

By the end of high school, music had become my passion. Playing the trumpet, however, revealed a major character flaw. One day way back in junior high school, I got angry at not being able to play a piece of music correctly, and banged my trumpet on the music stand, putting a huge dent in the bell. My dad was not very happy about that because he had to really sacrifice to buy my trumpet. It makes me wonder why I had anger at such a young age. I got very angry at myself for doing that, didn't know why I did, and didn't like telling people when they asked about the big dent. As I look back, that was one of the first times I didn't feel good about myself.

I left high school with an excitement of going into music as a career. Other fields I enjoyed were astronomy and drafting. Sometimes as I think back on how my life has gone in music, I wished I had chosen one of the other two occupations. Then again, it may not have been any different, because of attitudes and mindsets that had already been engrained in me that would hold me back from being success oriented.

I committed my life to the ministry of music because I could express my faith through it, honor God, and believed that He would bless me for that decision. The problem was that I put God in a box, meaning I gave Him no other options for using me. I limited God, but didn't realize at the time what I was doing. I thought I was being spiritual. Do you get the picture here? I committed my life to a particular occupation with the purpose of honoring God, presuming that He would bless it, and at the same time limiting God by my own thinking.

I went into the music ministry with hardly any thought given to money, because it was engrained in me that money was not important, compared to being in "God's will." I was never told that a person can be a Christian and also strive to become successful. Success was associated only with money and material wealth, so I thought it was wrong and unspiritual to seek to be successful.

I was also never encouraged to save money. In fact, I grew up believing it was wrong to save because by doing so one wasn't trusting God. Matthew 6:19 was often quoted. "Do not lay up for yourselves treasures upon earth, where moth and rust destroy, and where thieves break in and steal." Verse 21 says, "For where your treasure is, there will your heart be also." No distinction was made between *saving* and *treasuring*. There is a big difference! I believe now that it is okay for Christians to make a lot of money and save, if there is a willingness to give it all up. Refusing to let go of it is treasuring. The issue is, are you hoarding it for yourself, or using it to benefit people, ministries, and other worthwhile causes?

Goal setting was not something that was encouraged. Rather, I was told that if God wanted something to happen, it would happen.

I got these mindsets mostly from the "circle of Christians" with whom I associated. I never was exposed to a successful, goal-oriented Christian.

I came out of high school with no clearly defined purpose. My parents encouraged me to get a teaching degree, as something to fall back on. That advice has proven to be very valuable. There have been times when, without teaching, I would probably have had to find whatever I could, maybe at a low wage. On the other hand, as I got into teaching, it became very apparent that this profession was not a good "fit" for me.

When I had vocational counselling I never gave serious consideration to questions like, "What kind of money do I need to live on?" or "Based on my abilities and desires, what kind of career should I pursue?" I didn't see a need for it anyway because I was just going to follow "God's will."

Although I didn't realize it at the time, I was already beginning to develop negative strongholds[1]. Negative strongholds are destructive habits, attitudes, or mindsets that have a grip on us, and have become so much a part of our subconscious character, that they hold us back in defeat and mediocrity, where we cannot experience a life of victory and happiness. Look at II Corinthians 10:4-5:

"*For the weapons of our warfare are not of the flesh, but divinely powerful for the destruction of fortresses.* (Some translations use the word 'strongholds.') *We are destroying speculations and every lofty thing raised up against the knowledge of God, and we are taking every thought captive to the obedience of Christ.*"

Sadly, I didn't recognize what was happening. Along with this, I grew up believing, and it was accepted as a normal state of think-

1 Some translations use the word "stronghold." The footnote on page 1958 of the Nelson Study Bible gives an excellent explanation of strongholds. "Overlooking ancient Corinth was a hill 1,857 feet high. On top of it was a fortress. Paul used that imagery as an illustration of the spiritual warfare he waged. He destroyed strongholds, cast down towers, and took captives. The fortress, towers, and captives represent the arguments, thoughts, and plans that Paul was opposing. Paul cast down all rationalizations. He took captive to the *obedience of Christ* every perception and intention of the heart that was against God. Our actions reveal our thoughts. We should not cling to thoughts that do not conform to the life and teachings of Christ. Paul did not walk according to the flesh or his worldly desires; instead he conquered the flesh. He explains his strategy in I Cor. 9:24-27. '*I discipline my body and bring it into subjection*.'" (Used by permission of Thomas Nelson Publishers Nashville, Tenn.)

ing, that a Christian should follow "God's will," instead of one's own aspirations. How could I go wrong? I didn't expect to be living a life of defeat and just barely getting by. Rather, I expected that God would cause everything to come together in a way that my life would be blessed and victorious.

The previous verse emphasizes how a person thinks. The problem was with the low self-esteem. Although I wanted to go in the direction in which I believed God was directing, I did not seek to excel in life. I did not value myself, nor did I believe that I had much to offer anyone else. Low self-esteem kept me from experiencing God's best for my life.

HOW ABOUT YOU?

1. What negative experiences did you have in childhood that you have never dealt with? Did they hold you back in life, and if so, how?
2. What was your early church experience like? Has it hindered you or helped you? How?
3. When you left high school, how did you feel about yourself? What mindsets did you have, and have they negatively impacted you later in life?

Chapter 2

A PRISONER OF WRONG THINKING

For most of my life I was in self-imposed captivity behind the bars of wrong thinking.

I was actually about to enter a very exciting ear of my life. After going to two years of community college, I transferred to San Diego State University in 1969. This was the age of the Vietnam War protests and school sit-ins. People were talking a lot about peace. A common chant was, "All we are saying is give peace a chance."

I was very actively involved in Campus Crusade for Christ. This was the first major turning point in my life. My Christian beliefs started to become relevant. Two years earlier, between high school and college, I had attended a conference at Arrowhead Springs, California, which at that time, was the international headquarters for Campus Crusade. Speakers were talking about the possibility of Christ coming in our generation and how to walk in the power of the Holy Spirit. As part of evangelism training, I got to share the *Four Spiritual Laws* not only on campus, but also on the beach with girls in bikinis. My Christianity was becoming not only relevant, but also fun!

During this time in my life, I had the privilege of being a member of a very growing, thriving church in San Diego. At this church I heard people talk about going to Mt. Ararat to look for Noah's ark. It was at this church where I discovered my spiritual gifts. All of this was a whirlwind of spiritual growth.

There also happened to be at this church, a large number of people that were successful, but also dedicated believers. This was something new to me; I had never been around people who were both spiritual and successful. It was making me start to ask questions about how spirituality and success were related, or were they? The people in this congregation were also living a very positive faith.

After graduation with a degree in music education and receiving my teaching certification in 1973, I started substituting in the San Diego Unified School System. I didn't have steady employment, nor was I looking for any. I was living with my parents and saw nothing wrong with that.

During this time I got a vision of starting a Christian conservatory of music with another gentleman. True, I was following my heart, but I was barely getting by. Remember, I had this mindset that ministry was more important than money.

Before the conservatory got off the ground, a series of events happened that put road blocks in the way. Although I was beginning to develop a goal orientation, I was not success-minded enough to persist in spite of obstacles. My low self-esteem combined with an attitude that told me to accept whatever happens as being the will of God. When some events started occurring that were working against us in starting the conservatory, I took it to mean that God didn't want it to happen, so I quit! I know now that quitting is a failure mindset. I had a dream, but a distorted view of God's will, low self-esteem, and a lack of success orientation got in the way. If my belief system had been different, maybe I would still be living in San Diego as the co-founder and director of a Christian conservatory of music, however, I am living a "what-if" life today.

Substitute teaching continued for a couple of years, but I had a lot of problems with classroom control. Now, I know that was because I was a substitute. I based my dislike of teaching on substituting, decided I really did not want to teach, so I didn't pursue a regular full-time position. I told myself that I would never teach again, no matter what.

My self-esteem came into play here because I *allowed* kids to walk all over me, treat me poorly, and give me a hard time. I took it personally, and figured there must be something wrong with me. If I had had a healthy self-esteem, I probably would have responded totally differently. I would have recognized that there are problems as a first-year teacher and taken steps to correct them, in order to have a successful and enjoyable experience in the classroom. It has come to my attention through counseling that people with low self-esteem do not establish emotional boundaries.

Instead, I just quit! Again, I was already developing a victim/failure mindset. Why, I don't really know, but I was already becoming a quitter. I am reminded of the saying, "Quitters never win, and winners never quit." After I quit, you could find me driving a route for a local candy distributor, so I went from college educated and potential teacher, to delivering candy in the space of 2-3 years, *by choice*. There was no passion for teaching, so I wasn't determined to make it work. As I stated earlier, there was no definite focus. Instead of rising above the circumstances to the balcony, I fell into the basement of defeat.

Finally, at the age of 26, after having several other low paying jobs unrelated to my field, I moved out of my parents' house and got an apartment. However, I was settling for less than what I wanted and was trained to do. I wasn't making things happen, because I didn't think I was supposed to make things happen if I was surrendered to God's will. Since college, I had already worked four different jobs, and only one of them related to music. I had a part-time choir director position at a small church for a short time.

Because I didn't like teaching, I was beginning to shift my focus to church music ministry. When I found out that a seminary in the northwest offered a degree in church music, I made plans to attend for the next two years.

Here I was in my late twenties starting all over again pursuing a new direction. I was following my heart, but my path would turn out to be a rerun of the past, with no clear focus on my goals.

Being single, I was content just having my basic needs met, and just barely getting by because no one else depended upon me. Obviously, I didn't have a mindset for developing a solid financial base for the future, in case I got married, had to provide for a family, or any other financial catastrophe.

I also was not learning from my failures. I was not being persistent and was not becoming a better individual. Instead, all of my failures were contributing to my low self-esteem, anger, and defeated mindset.

HOW ABOUT YOU?

1. Are you experiencing some negative consequences in the present resulting from not dealing with issues in your past?
2. Where might you be today if you had confronted them and brought them to a satisfactory resolution?

Chapter 3

LOW SELF-ESTEEM AND THE WILL OF GOD

It is not God's will for us to think lowly of ourselves because when we do, we also miss out on the opportunities He provides.

I moved from southern California to Portland, Oregon, in the middle of the winter of 1979. One of the first things I learned was not about church music, but how to drive on ice. The city was experiencing one of the worst ice storms in history. I was in a new city, and didn't know a soul. History was repeating itself because I was starting all over, again, but seminary was going to begin a transformation.

The first thing I remember is sitting in a biblical interpretation class discussing hermeneutics. A person doesn't hear that word in church. It's a long, fancy word that has to do with proper biblical interpretation, as the original, inspired men of God meant it to mean.

Before I continue with my story, let me state my convictions about biblical interpretation. I believe men inspired by the Holy Spirit have written the Bible. Why do I believe this? It was written by many inspired authors over a span of hundreds of years, but it has a central theme, and every prophecy up until now has been fulfilled. It is historically accurate. It has proven true in my life when properly interpreted and applied. This inerrant and infallible word of God is a reliable source to bring about change.

However, to properly interpret the Bible, the historical and cultural setting must be taken into account. The themes of the individual books and to whom they were written must also be considered. Last, but just as important, it is essential to know the context of specific verses. There are dozens of opinions, but in order to see the truth of God's Word, it must be interpreted according to these principles. II Peter 1:20-21 says:

"*But know this first of all, that no prophecy of Scripture is a matter of one's own interpretation, for no prophecy was ever made by an act of human will, but men moved by the Holy Spirit spoke from God.*"

Learning these principles of interpretation was the first step in redirecting my thinking. It would prove to be more valuable than any instruction that I would receive in church music.

I immediately got involved in music, not only in seminary, but also in the Portland area. Providentially, a church found out about me coming to seminary through the music department chairman. I was on paid staff for most of the time in Portland.

It was an overall positive experience at this church, except for one time when I got angry, and felt it was necessary to apologize before the congregation. That was very difficult! It made me begin to wonder why, as a Christian, I had an anger problem. I felt very guilty about it. Here I was a seminary student. I mean, wasn't I supposed to be more righteous than the rest of the Christians? I am not being sarcastic here because I really truly believed that at the time.

In seminary I had the privilege of studying under a professor who was a former musical director at Hanna-Barbera Television in Hollywood. He was the composer of the *Flintstones* theme song. This was another time I was exposed to someone who was very successful, but also a very dedicated believer in the Lord.

At seminary I ran for and got elected to the student body office of music chapel leader. As I have learned more and more about low self-esteem, I think I did that to satisfy mine and my need to be recognized. You see, I have learned that part of low self-esteem is having an inferiority complex, so that you want to gain recognition and a feeling of superiority.

Aside from seminary, I dated several women and was very jealous of other men dating or even hanging out with women who I liked. I didn't think much of myself and wanted someone in my life who valued me. Low self-esteem severely hampered my dating relationships. The potential loss of friendships had a very negative and emotional effect upon me. In addition, there was the pressure of "getting connected" to someone due to the attitude in many churches that preferred staff members to be married.

Seminary began to turn my life around in two ways. The first, which I have already mentioned, is proper biblical interpretation. The other way, which was related to this, was developing new thinking about the will of God.

Up until seminary it was engrained in me that God has only one vocation for a person, only one right person to marry, and I even heard it carried to the ridiculous that God has a particular car to buy. I started wondering why God would care about what kind of car I drive. Why would He be concerned with where I live, or what I do to make a living, as long as it is moral, legal, and can glorify Him. I do believe that God, at times, puts people in a particular place for a reason, but isn't He more concerned with who I am in character, than what I do, or who I marry? If my heart is right, I will seek to glorify Him in whatever I do. I will "bloom where I am planted."

I heard people say that if I did not find God's specific plan for my life, or wandered out of His "perfect will," then God would not bless my life. Maybe for some people this teaching works, but it sure messed me up. I believe it slowed me down from accomplishing my potential and moving ahead in life. It caused confusion and frustration. Every time trials came into my life, I would wonder if I was in God's will. It was based on fear, not grace. When I was raised, this was the traditional view and still is today for some.

Does finding God's will mean greater blessing and happiness? Let's use marriage as an example. Two people have found each other. They both believe that God brought them together. They both think, "You are the one God has for me," without taking much time to find out about each other's pasts. After marriage and several years down the road, they discover that both of them have hurts and emotional baggage that has never been dealt with. To make matters worse, they don't know how to communicate. These two Christian people who believe they married their "Mr. or Mrs. God's Will," wonder why they are having so many problems.

In seminary I read a book entitled, *Decision Making and the Will of God (A Biblical Alternative to the Traditional View)*, by Garry Friesen. This author refers to what I have talked about as trying to find a dot within a circle of God's moral and biblical will. After reading this book, I came to the realization that sometimes God gives me more latitude in doing His will than I give myself. If the contexts of verses dealing with God's will are carefully examined, it will be discovered that most of the time they deal with developing a Godly character. God is more concerned with who I am, than what I do. His will is clearly revealed in Scripture. I do not believe that Christians need to spend half of their lives, like I did, trying to discern God's will. Just read His Word, and do it! I have discovered that the three words, "just do it," can change my life, and my relationship with God and others.

I now have so much freedom knowing that God is not going to bring calamity into my life if I am not "in His will." In fact, I am hard pressed to find in Scripture a direct connection between God's will and a specific vocation. Doesn't it make more sense to choose vocations that enable us to utilize our full potential for His glory? I am not saying that a person should never be available and obedient for God to use in any way He chooses. What I am saying is that sometimes people can spend so much time trying to figure out what God's will is, that they may not be using the intelligence, abilities, and spiritual gifts that God has given them. That is why I am writing this book. I did not look to see if it was a dot in the circle. I enjoy writing. I believe I have ability in this area and that my book has the potential to glorify God by helping a lot of people.

Let's get back to my story. After graduation I remained in Portland for several months and waited for the "call of God." I never was really clear on what constitutes a call. I have heard several views on the subject. One pastor once said that it is a call on the telephone to come be our pastor. Others have said that a person will have peace about something. Another way to think of it is, if there is a need in some area, and a person has a desire and burden to fill that need, then that is a call. With me, I needed a job, and I wasn't going to wait around when I needed to put food on the table.

Several contacts were made about music positions. None of them materialized. One of the churches turned me down just because I was single, and they told me that in a letter. That made me begin thinking that if I was going to fulfill my dream, I needed to be married. I could have taken the church to task on that issue because I knew that was not right, but I believed it would not have been the "Christian thing to do." I just let it go, maybe in large part due to my low self-esteem.

One job in Yakima, Washington looked promising. The position was for an administrator at a Christian school. Here I was, vacillating again. I used to teach, didn't like it, went to seminary to pursue church music and was once again looking into an educational position. But because no church music positions were opening up (or maybe I wasn't aggressively going after them), and at the time, I considered administration to be one of my strengths, I seriously looked into it. I would not have to be in the classroom that much. Even so, it was not what I went back to school to do. I wasn't focused.

I was actually very confused about the concepts of "God's will," and "the call." These are two misunderstood teachings that have caused more confusion and frustration among Christians than anything else.

Did I settle for less than what I really wanted? I believe I did, but I needed a job, and was this mindset related to my low self-esteem? I think it may have been because in situations like this I would usually settle for whatever came along. I did not think highly enough of myself to go after what I really desired.

The job in Yakima did go through, so I packed my belongings into a U-haul and headed there, which was about a three hour drive. The past was repeating itself, again. I was still single, moving into another strange town, not knowing anyone, starting over again in another vocation, and still just barely getting by.

A pattern was being established which would be difficult to break. I was around 30 at the time, a time when most people have established careers with solid incomes. I have found through this that it doesn't matter where you go or what you do with your life, when you take the same emotional baggage and mindsets with you, things will not change. To see change in our circumstances, we must change our thinking. God was beginning to work on my thinking, as you will see as you further follow my story. God was beginning to break the strongholds of my past.

When I left Portland, I was still thinking inside my box of a belief system that had held me back in life. I believed then that if I was really going after what I wanted, persistently, it was resisting God's will. The lid on the box was gradually beginning to open. I now believe that it is okay to hold out for what I really want, as long as I am open to God redirecting my path.

How does self-esteem relate to God's will? In my case, I took whatever came along. I did not think highly enough of myself and my abilities and interests to pursue God's best for my life. I wan not goal oriented. Now, with my rising self-esteem, I am moving in directions that enable me to make the most of myself and make a positive difference in the lives of other people. I am doing things that will accomplish that end. Writing this book is one of them. At the same time, I am always open to God's leading.

HOW ABOUT YOU?

1. Have there been times when you "let something go," but realized later you should have done something about it? What kind of effect has it had on your self-esteem?
2. As you look back on your life, do you see things that were problems, but at the time you did not consider them as problems?

Chapter 4

LOW SELF-ESTEEM AND SUCCESS

The lower my self-esteem, the smaller my goals. The smaller my goals, the less I move ahead in life.

Here I was in Yakima, Washington in 1979. I didn't know a soul. It was a very small town compared to San Diego and Portland. Located in dry, central Washington, I definitely would not feel the cool ocean breezes. There were four seasons, including very hot summers and cold, snowy winters. There was no smog and no congested freeways. It would turn out to be a really nice place to live.

With my music background, I was concerned that there would not be much going on in music and the arts but was pleasantly surprised to learn that this community had a symphony orchestra. A few months later I was sitting way up in the cheap five-dollar seats attending a concert.

Let me go back to my first day arriving in the city. I was in for a very unpleasant surprise when I came into the Christian school office. Upon introducing myself to the school secretary, I immediately was informed that I would be a teacher, not the administrator, because of budget restrictions. I was not told there was a change. Talk about a blow to my self-esteem.

Obviously, I was very hurt by this. I had relocated and found out that I didn't have the job I came for. To make matters worse, these people were Christians; I felt deceived and insignificant. My attitude was one of unwilling acceptance. Acceptance based on

God's will, so to resist would be wrong? Self-esteem can be measured in part by how much (fill in your own words), you are willing to put up with. I think it was a combination of the two. It left me with no clear sense of direction.

If that situation happened today, I would have said to the pastor, "We need to talk." I would tell him that he had not been honest with me, and I expect to have the job I was told I would have.

It comes down to this: acceptance or assertiveness. That can depend upon one's view of God's will, and one's level of self-esteem. When people have low self-esteem, they allow others to walk all over them and just accept what life dishes out to them. It kept me from asserting myself to receive what I truly wanted and what God had in store for me. In my case, I had to have a job, but I should have at least expressed my displeasure to the pastor. Instead, I just accepted it like nothing happened. This was caused by my low self-esteem. It also resulted in more anger and frustration building up inside me.

This gets to the subject of having options. If I had had options, I could have told the pastor that I was not going to work there because of the way I was treated. Would that have been "the Christian thing to do?" Obviously at the time, I felt it wasn't. *If* this was God's will, this must be the way it was supposed to happen, however, my low self-esteem determined my response to the situation. I believe it is a matter of providing for our basic needs, and hopefully, enjoying what we are doing.

A phrase commonly used today is "Follow your heart." What would you really do if you had choices not controlled by money? Is that opposite of God's will? Some Christians might say it is. I don't necessarily think so. It could be that sometimes God's will for us is to follow our heart.

Ironically, this job came to an end before the conclusion of the school year because of further budget cuts. Here I was without any job, again. God and I had a big conversation! If He wanted me to stay in Yakima, I asked Him to make it clear to me.

About this time, something happened in Yakima that not only put my life on hold, but everyone else's. Mt. St. Helens erupted on May 18, 1980, and spread ash all over the city. Everyone spent about the next month cleaning it up. I am not saying that this had anything to do with God giving me a sign. It didn't. It definitely, however, was a once in a lifetime experience. Yakima was referred to as the "ash hole of the nation." No joke!

Shortly after this, I walked into one of the local music stores, where they had just finished vacuuming ash out of all the pianos. Remember, I had asked God for an indication as to whether or not I should stay? I assume by the providence of God that, in talking to the store personnel, the conversation turned to the band rental program, and my background in music education. A few days later I was hired as the store's band department manager. I also ended up doing some private teaching. This job lasted three years and gave me steady income.

This situation of coming to Yakima, only to have the job be something different, and ending so soon, begs the question of whether it was even God's will to begin with. My thinking is, it was not the job that was His will; it was getting me to the city for a greater purpose. God places us at times in a particular place for a specific reason.

In Yakima, I got married. I also got involved in the Amway business. These were both radical changes for me. People have lots of thoughts about this business. What I saw were some professing Christians who were also millionaires with lifestyles of freedom to do whatever they wanted. It started to create within me a yearning to be successful. I wanted that type of life, and believe it could have been a new beginning for me, but I still had mindsets from my past. After several years I got out of the business because I wasn't making any money at it, but I also couldn't figure out how to be a committed Christian and successful too. I will talk about success and spirituality in chapter 9.

I was no longer at the music store, and I started drawing unemployment checks. During this time a Christian said to me that being without work was a chance to minister to people. That was like justifying that it was okay or even spiritual, to be unemployed.

For the first time in my life, I began to realize that I didn't need to do only music. Remember, way back at the beginning when I committed my life to music? Up until this point I had the idea that if I did something different, then God would not bless my life, but music clearly was not paying the bills. The bottom line was to provide for a family, and I now was in a position where I had to do whatever it took to do that.

I looked into some local jobs and did a job search through a Christian job search organization. Primarily, I looked for church music or teaching positions. Even with all of the problems, teaching was something I was trained to do, so I did not want to close the door on it. The other deciding factor was not wanting to move far away from the immediate family and relatives.

I accepted a job in the Los Angeles area. Here I was on my way, again, to another city. When most people move to different cities and states, it is considered a move up in life. For me, it was to start all over again.

A big part of moving ahead is learning from our failures, and I was a very slow learner. But can that be called failure? That is all in the attitude. At the time, I accepted it as part of life. As I look back on it, it was not failure. Failure is when you get knocked down and don't get back up. Experiencing God's best is bouncing back and continuing to move forward.

In contrast to this, however, my low self-esteem was a major roadblock in the path to plowing ahead, and I didn't consider myself moving forward. I just had to have a job.

HOW ABOUT YOU?

1. Have there been times when you didn't confront a situation because you thought it wasn't "the Christian thing to do?" Looking back on it, do you wish you had?
2. Have you had any "what-if" experiences? How have they made you feel about yourself, and do you feel they possibly changed the course of your life?
3. Are you content with accepting whatever happens?

Chapter 5

THE BONDAGE OF MEDIOCRITY

Many Christians live in a rut of mediocrity because they don't seek God's best.

California here I come again. This time my destination was Los Angeles. It's referred to as the City of Angels. I often said it was a nice place to visit, but I wouldn't want to live there. There are lots of things to do and places to go, if one has the patience to put up with all of the traffic. San Diego would become a peaceful haven when life got too hectic in Los Angeles.

My life was being controlled by low self-esteem and the need for money. I was back into teaching, something I did not enjoy, in another new location. I was making changes in my life because I had to, not by choice. I had no options. I was not being able to follow my heart, and to make the most of myself and my abilities.

The mindset and financial resources to be independent and self-reliant were never part of me. I never was able to make things happen, so I would have to rely on others much of the time, even for basic needs. I used to think that "making things happen," was taking matters into my own hands, "running ahead of God," and not "waiting on God." These were the phrases I would hear Christians use that made me feel unspiritual if I didn't follow them. I believe now that we should use everything at our disposal to accomplish good things for our lives and for His glory.

My job at the Christian school involved band, choir, and classroom music. Because of my seminary education, I also was responsible for a Bible class. I was taking work home with me. Welcome back to the world of teaching! Immediately, I began having problems with anger and classroom control. What made it worse was I didn't know why I had so much of a problem with anger, or how to deal with it. I just knew it was making my teaching experience miserable. It was quite stressful. For all of this, I was getting paid only one thousand dollars a month!

While at the school, I found out about a job for a part-time music minister at a Baptist church in Long Beach. I was hired. It was a fairly good sized, rapidly growing congregation, and they had multiple services. Even though it required a long drive on the freeways, things were improving. My heart's desire was being fulfilled.

About one year later, I learned that the school was not going to renew my contract. That was not surprising because of the problems I was having. Remember, I said earlier that when you change your location, if you take the same unresolved issues with you, you will experience the same results. It has been said that insanity is doing the same things over and over, but expecting different consequences. By that definition, I guess I lived a life of insanity.

Fortunately, I found another job for the next school year at a Christian school close to the church. It was even a longer drive, but paid considerably more money, so I began to make a fairly decent income with both jobs combined. For me, I was doing well, but compared to what? Was living in an apartment and living from month to month doing well?

Compared to where I had been, I was doing better than average, but what is average? It was said by someone in the Amway business that average is the best of the worst, and the worst of the best. It appeared, however, that things were moving in a positive direction toward my dream of getting on staff at a large church.

I had been teaching at the school for not even one school year, when I was told I would be terminated. I wasn't surprised because it was like the same song, second or third verse. Angry reactions to misbehaving students in the classroom was again the problem. I did not know how to control students and "keep my cool." Plus,

I really did not like teaching, so I wasn't determined to make it work.

No one ever took me aside and said, "Look, John, you have some problems that you need to deal with." With my self-esteem being so low, however, I probably would not have welcomed any help. My attitude was that I wasn't suited to teaching. As I look back on it, the problem was largely my angry, reactive temperament.

After about nine months I thought my position as music minister was going well. I had an adult choir at a strong, vibrant church, which I believed had a real future for ministry. One night after an evening service, with no warning I was called into the pastor's office, and with no explanation, I was told that the church no longer wanted me. My self-esteem was so low, that I didn't question their decision; I just accepted it. That, of course, was devastating to me! It had taken so long to get into a position like this. To be told this by a church, by Christians, was almost more than I could deal with.

It was a week later when I made an appointment with the pastor to discuss why this happened. (At least, this time, I talked to the pastor about it. I never did talk to the pastor in Yakima.) He said it was because I had offended some people. Offended some people? I mean, I am not saying that should be taken lightly, but to fire me over it, without even talking to me? I could not believe it! Couldn't they have taken me aside and given me an opportunity to make things right? This is the Christian thing to do. I called some people whom I thought I might have offended, and everyone said there really was no problem. I did what I could do. It took me a L-O-N-G time to get over that.

Both the church and teaching jobs were history. I was totally without work, with no unemployment benefits, and no idea what I would do. I knew I would not do classroom teaching again. In spite of my heart being broken by church music, I still had a passion for it. My belief system once again told me to just accept everything that happens as being "God's will, without questioning it."

People can learn a lot about themselves by how they handle setbacks. First of all, they can either get bitter or better. They can stay down and not get back up, or they can use the setback to bounce back even higher into the future. People with low self-esteem take setbacks personally. They think there is something wrong with themselves. The problem lies in that they think too lowly of themselves. Setbacks should be used as springboards to propel us further toward our goals and dreams. One's attitude can determine one's altitude.

Now, where would I even begin to look for work? In a situation like this, I figured I needed to do whatever was necessary to generate as much income as possible, as quickly as possible, to put food on the table. It was my first experience going to a church and asking for assistance. It wasn't fun! I didn't want to have to ever ask for assistance again. Unfortunately, that would not be the case. Next, I started going to employment agencies to get some idea of what was available in line with my interests. Here, I was, a failure as a teacher with a dream of church music that had been denied me, but not trained to do anything else.

After quite some time, I took a job as a security guard because it required no experience. This job lasted three years, the first year of which was spent guarding a construction site in east L.A., not the most ideal environment. The other years I worked at a big distribution center. It was very stable work, but paid slightly above minimum wage. This was another blow to my self-esteem. I had a teaching degree and a master's degree in church music ministry, but was spending eight hours a day working in a guardhouse. A man does what a man has to do!

What is God's will in a case like this? God's will is that the family is provided for. Scripture makes it very clear; I didn't have to pray about it.

"But if anyone does not provide for his own, and especially for those of his household, he has denied the faith, and is worse than an unbeliever." I Timothy 5:8. Sometimes I think Christians can spend so much time praying and seeking God's will, that we are not out doing what needs to be done. God has given us intelligence, common sense, and abilities, and expects us to utilize these things. We can and should seek His wisdom because James 1:5 says:

"*But if any of you lacks wisdom, let him ask of God, who gives to all men generously and without reproach, and it will be given to him.*" However, I think it is possible to be so wrapped up in trying to find "God's perfect will," that His will is missed completely.

There was a new Christian school of fine arts which was starting in the Los Angeles area. It was like the one for which I had a dream in San Diego, but quit. I played in a jazz band and an orchestra that backed up Christian drama productions. I also did some private teaching, which brought in a meager amount of income. A private tutoring center was near by, so I also did tutoring in basic math and reading.

A dream I had had for a long time was to teach music at the college level. I applied for and was able to get hired at the evening school at a local university. My thinking was beginning to become focused on going after what I really wanted, and doing whatever it took to realize my goals.

The private teaching and night courses brought in tidbits of side income. I was having fun, but none of this had any future. On the other hand, I was following my heart, and was basically content with that.

Therein lies a problem. I was complacent about not getting ahead in life. There is a concept of contentment in the Bible, spoken of in Philippians 4:11, and I Timothy 6:6-8:

"*Not that I speak from want; for I have learned to be content in whatever circumstances I am.*" (Phil.) "*But godliness actually is a means of great gain, when accompanied by contentment. For we have brought nothing into the world, so we cannot take anything out of it either. And if we have food and covering, with these we shall be content.*" (I Tim.)

So, what is this contentment of which the Bible speaks? Does it mean having everything, having a relatively easy life free of a lot of problems? Is it the idea of not needing much money, and only having basic needs met? Is it contentment and spiritual to *not* want an abundant, prosperous life? I thought for a long time that it was not spiritual to have a "dream list." That is another reason why I could not reconcile my Christian life with the Amway business.

In John 10:10 Christ says, "... *I came that they might have life, and might have it abundantly*." What does abundance mean? Whether it means material things, or an abundance of the "fruit of the Spirit," or seeing people come to know Christ, I wasn't experiencing any of the above. No matter how one might define the word, I was missing out on the abundant life.

I was a Christian involved in numerous church activities and programs, but was living a defeated and mediocre life, and not making a positive difference in the lives of others. I would hear people get up in church and tell about winning souls and how victorious their lives were, but would ask myself the question, "What's wrong with me? How come my life is not like that?" It added to my feeling of guilt.

No one ever asked me to be a leader in church or serve on a board, but I never volunteered either. Low self-esteem caused me to not step forward, yet at the same time, I wished someone would have asked me to do something because I craved recognition and a sense of value. Then I felt more lowly of myself, and the cycle was reinforced and perpetuated.

The purpose of my life was not being fulfilled. I didn't want to be just working and involved in activities. If I wasn't making a difference in the lives of others, then what was the point? At this time in my life, if I could have started my life over, I would have. I now see three major reasons why my life went like it did: low self-esteem, a distorted view of God's will, and no goal orientation and focus.

When I was let go at the church with no warning or explanation, I thought there must be something wrong with me, but really didn't know how it related to God's will. I do know that it is His will for His children to be reconciled to one another. Do I believe that I was a victim of a church violating this principle? Yes, I do!

Was it His will that I was terminated at the school? I do not know, but I do know the reason. It was because I could not handle myself well working with students. This had to do with unresolved issues of anger and classroom control.

To be successful in life, it is absolutely imperative that one deals with the issues that stand in the way. You and I are not responsible for how we were raised, but we are responsible for what we become. I believe my life could have been totally different today if I had dealt with these hurdles earlier.

Along side all of this, I had developed a belief that prayer and Bible reading would make all of my problems go away, but that was not the case. Now about 20 years later, I have come to realize precisely what the problem was, which I will discuss in a later chapter. Another thing with which I struggled were Bible verses that people threw at me, which were supposed to give me comfort and help, but only made me more exasperated.

An opening came up for a music director at the new church I was now attending, and I applied for it. As a church member with a degree and experience in church music, I figured it looked very promising. It turned out that I was not even talked to, and the church hired some big name composer from the outside. That made me feel so left out, with another major blow to my self-esteem. I resented the church leadership for totally ignoring one of their own members, but didn't speak up about it because I thought I would come across as victimized.

Whatever the case, I should have talked to people, and if I had had good self-esteem, I am sure I would have. This situation needed to be addressed so that anger would not fester within me. It was very difficult working with the new music minister — the guy from the outside. I decided that if the church where I was a member didn't want me, then what church would.

My low self-esteem resulted in me not wanting to confront the church leaders. Yes, I was very angry about it! Right on the heels of being let go at the other church, this happened! I thought maybe there was something wrong with the way people perceived me. Actually, what was wrong was how I thought of myself. There was the issue of God's will again. Was it or wasn't it? Maybe it was church politics. Only God knows. There is a saying that "life is not fair." Unfortunately, in my experience, local churches have caused much of the unfairness.

In 1990, a move was made back up to Washington State for family reasons. Also, things were not going well in L.A., and there was no good reason to stay. However, I had nothing planned in Yakima Valley for income, and I would be (Yep, you have heard the phrase several times already!) starting all over, again, and this time at the age of forty-one.

Within about two months, I learned of a music director position open at a Presbyterian church about fifteen miles away. I applied for it, had an interview, and got the position. That was a change for me; I had gone to Baptist churches all of my life, but the Baptist church was the one that let me go without any warning. So if the Baptists didn't want me, the Presbyterian's got me. By then, I was freed enough from my "boxed in Baptist only" belief of earlier years to move into a different denomination.

This church was a very positive experience for me. It had a pipe organ, with a good organist. Occasionally, I even hired musicians from the local symphony orchestra to accompany the choir. It was a great time, especially after what I had been through previously with churches. What happened at the two churches in L.A. did not go unnoticed by God. He knew I had been treated unjustly. I believe that it was no coincidence that this position opened when it did.

Because of the meager income from this part-time position, I had to secure other employment. I worked as a telemarketer. Then

I learned the construction trade and built manufactured homes for five years. After that, I became a state certified driver's education instructor at a commercial driving school. I enjoyed that and received good reviews from my students. People change over time. I wasn't having all of the problems from earlier years, but I am sure it had something to do with the students wanting to be there.

Since I had to reactivate my teaching certification to teach driver's education, and enjoyed teaching, I intended to make use of it. Because I had sustained a hearing loss (maybe from five years of construction noise), I did not go back into teaching music; that would be too noisy for my ears to handle. I became, of all things, a substitute teacher. This time though I determined to make it work.

Every day in the classroom before students came in, for several months, I sat in the chair and practiced visualization. I formed mental images of my handling situations in a controlled, calm fashion, and pictured myself being the kind of teacher I wanted to be. Visualization works! Performers use it. It is used in sports. Olympic athletes make use of it. It literally transformed me as a classroom teacher, but I still have to give conscious attention, at time, to not "blowing up" in the classroom, when the students are particularly hard to deal with.

I was at the Presbyterian church for ten years. Wow! I was a driver's education instructor for six years. As I write this, I am in my sixth year of substitute teaching. Amazing! These things have given me a long-term income, thanks to my dad's advice over thirty years ago, to get a teaching degree as something on which to fall back. Without this I don't know what I would have done.

Presently, I am attending a church, working with two other people who have music degrees, having a wonderful time. Recently, I was invited to play in a brass quartet, which has been a dream of mine for a long time. God is fulfilling the desires of my heart.

I am singing with a more free tone quality. Trained singers reading this will know what I mean. Simply put, as I have become less and less bound by the emotional issues of my past, I have become more free and expansive in the physical parts of the body that concern vocal production. Also, I am focused more on what I am singing, instead of my problems. No longer am I singing only about Jesus, but I am singing to Jesus, and I am singing the emotions of the words, not just the words.

This is not the end of my story. I am, by God's grace, pulling out of forty years of limiting mindsets. It is not easy to do in my mid fifties. By His grace I have a lot of years left, and it is never too late to change. I am goal oriented, and I am focused on becoming an influential person for God. The best of me is yet to be.

Limiting mindsets are manifested in several ways, including these three:

- An emotional reaction to another person's behavior or to a disturbing situation
- An addiction
- A negative mental attitude that is used to cope with people or adversity.

These things not only stand between God and us, but destroy relationships, make us think less of ourselves, or all three. Can Christians have these problems? They can, and they do.

Take the following self-test to determine to what degree you are limited, or have been liberated, in your thinking. A "No" answer to any of the questions may indicate a limiting attitude.

1. Do you feel the freedom to associate with people and churches of different denominations?
2. Do you feel the freedom to worship with churches that have a different form of worship?
3. Do you have an attitude of acceptance, for the sake of spiritual unity, of different musical instruments and styles of music used in worship?
4. Can you be yourself and fulfill your goals, without being bound by the expectations of others?
5. Can you set goals without wondering if it is God's will?
6. Do you move forward with goals and decisions, even if the money is not available?

7. Can you accept people of all races, lifestyles, and economic levels?
8. Do you believe that God loves you and wants to bless your life?
9. Do you think thoughts of sufficiency?
10. Do you think positive thoughts about others?
11. Do you accept people where they are, with their problems?
12. Do you claim God's blessing and favor upon your life every day?
13. Do you choose to be happy, regardless of circumstances or other people's reactions to you?
14. Are you free from tradition, or the saying, "We have always done it this way."
15. Can you confront negative situations without losing control of your emotions?
16. Can you deal with negative situations without destroying relationships?

I used to have a "No" answer in thirteen of these areas, but God, by His loving mercy and grace, has been turning the "No's" into "Yes." I have seen more spiritual growth take place in my life in the past six years, than throughout my entire Christian life, because I am getting rid of negative strongholds of the past through transformed thinking.

HOW ABOUT YOU?

1. Has your belief system limited you or liberated you?
2. Do you have any attitudes that are holding you back from accomplishing your goals?
3. Are there any thoughts or mindsets that are impeding your effectiveness and positive influence in the lives of others?
4. Is there anything that is hindering your walk with the Lord?
5. How did you do on the Self Test? You can use this test for periodic self-evaluation, or apply these questions to specific circumstances or issues.

Chapter 6

THE BONDAGE OF RELIGIOUS TEACHING

I "waited on God" so much, I never went anywhere.

To be very blunt, much of my belief system had not worked. I had read my Bible and prayed for years, but still had the same problems of low self-esteem, anger, and many other issues. Remember, as I stated in the introduction, I am talking about strongholds of which Christians may not even be aware, which hinder victory, spiritual maturity, and prevent us from moving ahead in life.

While I was at the Presbyterian church, things really started to unravel, and I knew I needed help. All these decades of unresolved issues and pent up anger started coming to a head, especially at home. When it got so bad that I was considering staying over night at the pastor's house one Saturday evening because of an uncontrolled anger issue at home, that was more than I wanted to admit. To make matters worse, I would have to be up on stage at church the very next morning directing the music. I was wearing a big mask. This pushed me over the edge. Even though I was a music worship leader, at times I couldn't concentrate on worship. I poured my life into my music ministry, but by this time in my life, there wasn't much music left to pour. I resigned my position at the church for several reasons, one of which was to get my life together and on track. I had to take the time that I was putting into my ministry, and use it to deal with the problems in my life.

So, up to this point, how did my life end up like this? Besides all of the unresolved issues that I have already talked about, I am a living example of how religious jargon void of meaning, and Scripture verses taken out of context and not properly understood or applied, can mess up one's thinking and do damage for life. Hebrews 12:1 tells us:

"Therefore, since we have so great a cloud of witnesses surrounding us, let us also lay aside every encumbrance, and the sin which so easily entangles us, and let us run with endurance the race that is set before us."

In my experience, religious jargon and the misinterpretation of particular Bible verses were an encumbrance. This verse tells me that I am supposed to lay aside anything that keeps me from seeing victory or slows down my progress toward spiritual growth.

I decided to re-examine verses that have been a source of frustration and confusion. God is not the author of confusion. I Corinthians 14:33 states, "For God is not a God of confusion, but of peace…" Have you ever been led to believe, like I was, that certain things will happen in your life if you follow the teaching of a specific verse taken out of context, or how someone says it should be interpreted, and then when these things do not happen you think less of yourself or start to question your faith? When I started to "lay aside" the usual interpretation of particular verses and saw the truth in context, I began to be liberated from the bondage of confusion, and it was no longer an "encumbrance" to running "the race that is set before me."

There are four verses that I most clearly recall, which were constantly thrown at me by well meaning Christians. These views are still held today by many.

1. Romans 8:28

Most Christians know that this verse is one of the most often quoted. "*And we know that God causes all things to work together for good to those who love God, to those who are called according to His purpose.*"

This verse was quoted to me when some adversity came into my life, to the point to where I became very angry about it. The implication was that something better would happen. Everyone always thought of it in relationship to circumstances, but look at the context closely.

The overall context of Romans 6-8 has to do with victory over our sins, temptations, and habits. The next verse in particular (8:29) speaks of being "conformed to the image of His Son." The entire context emphasizes character development. When people used it to mean circumstances, it was a major source of confusion. If things didn't get better, I thought that maybe I didn't love God, or wasn't fulfilling His purpose, which in turn, caused a guilt trip. When I realized God causes all things to mold my character, I no longer had confusion and guilt. In fact, it made me love God more. God, of course, can bring good out of bad, but in my opinion, this is not the verse to use to support this teaching.

2. Matthew 6:33

"*But seek first His kingdom and His righteousness, and all these things shall be added to you.*" These things" appear, from the context, to refer back to the basic needs of food and clothing mentioned earlier in the passage. If I was seeking God's kingdom and righteousness, why was I always broke, even to the point of having to ask for assistance? It brought more confusion.

From this verse I somehow formed a connection between the spiritual and economic level of a person. I was told to trust God one day at a time, which is all right, but it was never balanced out with the importance of financial planning for the future. If I was sincerely seeking God and His righteousness, I didn't believe that I should ever be in financial need. Christians always quoted this verse when talking about God's provision. It made me feel poorly of myself, and it made me question my commitment to God.

Confusion was further caused by never understanding the concept of the "kingdom of God." A verse I just started memorizing, defines this. It is Romans 14:17. "*For the kingdom of God is not eating and drinking, but righteousness and peace and joy in the Holy Spirit.*" I decided that "these things" more likely refers to righteousness, peace, and joy. It took away the confusion I have had in making a connection between seeking God as a prerequisite for His provision.

3. II Corinthians 5:17

"*Therefore if any man is in Christ, he is a new creature; the old things passed away; behold, new things have come.*"

As I saw it, because I had Christ in my life, according to this verse, positive changes and victory were supposed to happen, but they didn't. So, sometimes I began to doubt my salvation, or began wondering if there was something wrong with my spiritual walk. I got the impression from hearing other Christians talk about this verse, that things like bad habits would just leave without much effort on my part. There is nothing in the context that indicates this as the meaning. There are people who have been delivered "overnight" from drugs, alcohol, and smoking, but this does not happen to everyone. Sometimes God may choose to take people through a healing process, which takes time and a lot of hard work.

When divine healing does occur, it shows the awesome power of God. A woman in the church I attend had tried everything to quit smoking for 30 years. Nothing had worked. One day a few months ago, she wrapped her arms around her chest, and spoke the words, "I command that this addiction leave my body, in Jesus' name, Amen." Three days later she woke up, told herself she was going to quit, and has not smoked since.

4. John 15:5

People would misquote this, and they still do today, to say "*Apart from me you can do nothing.*" This was misinterpreted that without Christ, we are incapable of doing anything, or we have no abilities or talents. Whatever happened to spiritual gifts? They quoted only half of the verse. This kind of teaching contributed to my low self-esteem. The entire verse reads, "*I am the vine, you are the branches; he who abides in Me, and I in him, he bears much fruit, for apart from me you can do nothing.*" It has to do with bearing fruit. That changes things considerably! As an intelligent being created in God's image, we are capable of many great accomplishments, but it is only another activity or program that will not bear the fruit of the Holy Spirit, or the fruit of souls won to the Lord, unless we abide in Christ.

Interpreting and applying verses according to the context is so critical for practical Christian living. The misquoting and misapplication of these four verses did more harm than good while I was growing up. This reinforced my distorted mindset.

II Timothy 2:15 exhorts us to "*Be diligent to present yourself approved to God as a workman who does not need to be ashamed, handling accurately the word of truth.*" This verse makes it clear that it is imperative that Scripture is properly interpreted. Matthew 13:23 makes a connection between properly understanding Scripture and bearing fruit. "*And the one on whom seed was sown on the good soil, this is the man who hears the word and understands it; who indeed bears fruit…*"

Religious jargon also contributed to my misconceptions. Some Christians continually used words and phrases without any explanation of their meaning, and I never asked for an explanation because I was just supposed to accept them as part of religious language. How many times, as a Christian, have you heard the following phrases?

- "Just turn it over to the Lord."
- "Just wait on God."
- "Don't run ahead of God."
- "Just listen to the still, small voice."
- "Just pray about it."

Do you know what these phrases mean? Before you go any further in reading this chapter, could you write out a one sentence definition of each of them?

People flippantly used the phrase, "Just turn it over to the Lord," as if everything would be all right. I took the phrase, "Just wait on God," to mean that I should not do anything until God gives the okay. How did I know when God was saying "Go?" The implication in my mind was to not plow ahead with persistence and dogged determination, so I didn't. Instead, I never aggressively went after what I wanted.

When people said, "Don't run ahead of God," I had no idea if I was getting in front of God. Maybe I was lagging behind! How did I know how fast God was walking or running? Now I know that I would rather have God holding me back than me holding Him back.

I honestly believe that the phrases I have just mentioned held me back in life because they reinforced the thinking that it was wrong to have my own goals, and move ahead as quickly as humanly possible to accomplish those goals. I was very confused! Now I believe that they refer to God's timing and sovereignty.

"Just listen to the still, small voice." This phrase was always very vague. It could mean different things to different people. Was it a person's conscience? Was it a literal voice? Was it a feeling? How does one know if it is really God talking? It could be Satan, or one's own desire.

The phrase I heard the most was, "Just pray about it." People came across as if it was some kind of cure-all and would make all of my problems just go away. I am not making light of prayer, but I would pray, pray and pray, and still have the same problems. I see now that when I prayed, I focused on the problems even more. That would further reinforce and imbed it in my mind. As a result, there was no victory. I was praying wrong!

There were also hymns that contained words in them that made me feel poorly of myself. One popular hymn, *Amazing Grace*, contains the word "wretch." The word means, "a deplorably unhappy or unfortunate person," or "a despicable or base person." Although I have done some very wretched things in my life, I do not or did not view myself as a wretched person. Another hymn I sang a lot growing up was, *At the Cross*. This hymn compares an individual to being a worm. These two hymns must have been composed by people with very low self-esteem. Being a worm reminds me of another passage of Scripture.

Colossians 2:23 mentions "self-made religion and self-abasement." If you look up the definition of "abasement" in a dictionary, you will find that it means, "humiliation, lowering of or loss of self-respect, or degradation." Sad to say, I have been around some Christians who have given me the impression that the less I think of myself, the more God will use me. We don't have to allow anything, including hymns, to make us think less of ourselves. We are very valuable to God. That is why He died for us. There is a saying that goes, "Are we soaring with the eagles or scratching with the chickens?"

With whatever teaching we have been raised the question is, "Does it work in practical, everyday life?" As I mentioned in the first part of this book, we are not talking about issues of divine inspiration, or who Jesus is, or salvation. Don't just accept something because it is the way you are supposed to believe. Is your life continually changing for the better? This begins by thinking correctly about God, others, and ourselves.

When I started recovery, I knew that the beliefs I had been told all of my life had not worked. That is why my life was so messed up. I was determined to make it work, even if it meant discarding my past belief system.

In my view, it all comes down to this. A belief system (meaning mindsets, attitudes, church teaching, and childhood programming), must be allowing one to move ahead in life. It must be making us into better individuals and strengthening our walk with God. It must be enabling us to serve God and others more effectively, and to bear fruit for Him. Does one's belief system work, or doesn't it?

INTRODUCTION TO THE NEXT SECTION

Now that I have given you my story, I am going to share with you how all this emotional and psychological baggage has impacted my present. I will be discussing things not normally mentioned in church, unless you happen to attend a church that has a recovery ministry. Therefore, if you are not involved in counseling or some type of support group, you will probably not have much exposure to, or discussion of, the problems I am going to mention.

I want to give you enough information to help you identify any problems that may exist in your life, along with some tools that may assist you in dealing with them. This book is not intended to be a substitute for professional counseling, nor can it be. Hopefully, however, it will spur you on more in that direction if you see the need for it in your own life. I am certainly no expert in the things about which I am going to talk, but I have gained much insight through my recovery which has helped me apply these concepts in my life.

I have provided a topical and extensive recommended reading list of books to which you can refer, at the end of this book. These books will help you in gaining more insight and help from authors who are experts in specific areas.

Chapter 7

A PRISONER OF THE PAST

"Get past your past."

The most compelling situation in my life was finding out why, especially as a Christian, I had all of these problems. I simply could not go on living happily with myself, and as a staff member at local churches without having some answers. I desperately needed to know the causes of my problems, and to get my life on track to seeing positive change.

Another compelling factor was how all of this was affecting my family life. I knew it was not supposed to be like it was, and was afraid of the potential negative consequences.

Everything in my life was just the opposite of what my belief system told me it should be. I either needed to change my beliefs or find out why mine weren't working.

Furthermore, my negative strongholds had become traps. Let's use low self-esteem as an example. One of the results of low self-esteem for me was living a life of mediocrity, which in turn led to thinking poorly of myself. This perpetuated the low self-esteem. It is a circle that goes around and around.

Low Self-Esteem

What is low self-esteem? First of all, it is not to be confused with humility. Humility is not thinking too highly of yourself. Low self-esteem is thinking too lowly of yourself. It is like me saying, "I am *just* a substitute teacher."

Christ is the ultimate example of humility when He washed the feet of the disciples. He didn't think when He did this, "Here I am, the Son of God, doing this lowly task." A person with low self-esteem would probably think this way.

How did low self-esteem affect my life? One, I was some what reserved. Two, I did not have a firm handshake. A handshake really does say a lot about how a person views himself. Three, I did not step forward when something needed to be done that I was capable of doing. Four, I was not relationship oriented, meaning, I was too much inside myself to think about building relationships with others. When I went to church functions, I would be the one standing around not talking to anyone, and when I did talk it was usually about myself. Five, when other people got chosen to do things that I knew I was qualified to do, I wondered why I didn't get selected. Six, I suffered from an inferiority complex. Others reaffirmed my sense of having nothing to offer. Seven, I was very defensive and could not take criticism well.

Low self-esteem definitely held me back in life, and I believe it has kept me from experiencing God's best. I limited God by how I viewed myself. I was not "going for the gold" because I considered myself worthy only of the bronze. This attitude reared its ugly head in job interviews, so I probably did not make a good impression on potential employers.

Some things that used to be acceptable to me because of low self-esteem, are no longer acceptable, like just barely getting by, or having no goals. In some respects I am less content now than I used to be. I desire to provide a better life for my loved ones, but I don't have the resources to do that, yet. God, through His grace, is beginning to do what I cannot do in a host of small ways.

Negative Attitude

I had a negative and defeated attitude. There are basically two types of people, positive-minded and negative-minded, and it is like being in two different worlds. Christianity is a very positive message and belief system when it is interpreted and applied biblically. Being a Christian and being consistently negative do not go together. Most people would probably consider themselves to be positive, but being negative may be exhibited in ways some times not thought of as being negative. Consider the following list of comparisons.

Negative Vs. Positive

1. Thinking of excuses why something cannot be done instead of thinking of creative ways it can be done.
2. Finding fault with someone or something instead of looking for the good in everything.
3. Bound by tradition instead of being open to change.
4. Blaming problems on others or circumstances instead of owning the problems and taking responsibility for them.
5. Holding back in fear and doubt, and making negative assumptions instead of moving ahead in faith and confident expectancy.
6. Using the words "can't," "impossible," or "hopeless," instead of refusing to even think these words.
7. Thinking poorly of others instead of holding other people in positive high regard.
8. Giving up instead of being persistent, and refusing to quit.
9. Viewing failure as an end in itself instead of seeing it as a springboard to greater success.
10. Focusing on the problems instead of dwelling on the possibilities and solutions.
11. Associating with negative people as opposed to positive people.
12. Having a victim, poor-me mindset instead of choosing to live in victory.
13. Getting distracted by petty things, and the expectations of others instead of keeping focused on goals and priorities.

14. Allowing bitterness and unforgiveness to get in the way of relationships instead of working hard at keeping relationships right with people.

People can choose to be positive or negative by how they think. Let me be very blunt! From my experience, I do not believe that God uses negative thinkers! Negative thoughts about ourselves, God, and others are limiting thoughts that hold us back from fully developing our God-given potential, and from being used in the lives of others. Positive thoughts allow God's power of possibilities and creativity to flow through us.

I was negative in most of these ways.

Codependency

Now, let's shift gears to another problem. After being at counselling for awhile, I started hearing the term "codependent." It took a long time for me to begin to understand codependency, but when I did, I took another step forward to becoming a better person. People often think of codependency in connection with living with someone who is addicted to drugs or alcohol, but it goes beyond that. I'm reading several books on the subject. I have learned that codependency is allowing one's attitudes and actions to be determined by the attitudes and actions of other people, events, and circumstances. In addition to this, one tries to control other people and circumstances. This was true in my case, and still is to some degree.

Added to this was my very low self-esteem and insecurity, which made me think that everything was my fault. To further compound the problem, I reacted to things in an angry manner. Anger is a symptom of codependency. This negatively impacted my family relationships, sometimes my work, my relationships with students in the classroom, and my interaction with other drivers on the road.

Codependency can be caused by religious upbringing and teaching that discourages the expression of one's feelings and problems, along with an acceptance of beliefs without questioning them, even if those beliefs are holding one back in life.

Something that was discussed quite a bit at counselling was the difference between reacting and responding. I have learned much of this through my classroom experience. *Reacting* is losing control of myself. *Responding* is taking control of a situation without losing control of myself. This was a step toward dealing with codependency.

Along with this, I had a victim/failure mindset. I had thoughts like, "Why did this happen to me?" I was continually thinking how life is not fair, but my thinking was actually worse than that. Over time, I began to tell myself that for some reason God had selected me to live a life of mediocrity, or a "settle for less just barely get by" existence. I used to go outside, raise my fist in the air, curse God, and ask, "God, I have served and been faithful to you all of my life. Why is my life like this?"

Anger

Anger is an emotion like happiness, joy, or sadness. People may express anger when they do not like someone or some situation. My problem began with repressed anger. I held it in for a long time, and eventually started exploding. This repression of anger was caused by not expressing myself. It also resulted from not dealing with unresolved issues that blocked my way in moving ahead. All of the things that have happened to me about which you have read, but were never resolved, built up inside me for decades. My anger needed to be released, and how it was released was very important.

Anger has so many different arenas of cause and affect. Before going to counselling, I did not know what was causing my anger, or how to deal with it.

Depression

Eventually, all of the problems of low self-esteem, negativity, codependency, and anger led to depression. I was depressed because I started to not like myself. I got down on myself, and it turned into a downward spiral. Being "stuck" in negative situations where I didn't see any way out also caused depression. It was made worse by the fact that I was a Christian with a false belief system. I knew my life was not supposed to be this way, but there was no victory. I began to view myself as a loser. It all became too overwhelming! I looked for help from God, but found no answers. I just couldn't cope any more, even though I was doing all of the things that "a good Christian" was told to do.

I got to where I really didn't see much reason to live. I began praying that God would take my life. Things got to be very hopeless and I felt helpless to do anything about it. Several times, I was so angry and depressed, I felt like getting into my car and driving it into a tree.

If you feel you are in depression, take note, and seek help. My former counsellor said, "Of all the mental illnesses, depression is the easiest to cure, but the most deadly."

Financial Bondage

On top of all that I have mentioned, I had financial bondage due to mindsets of the past. I had not saved money my entire life, except for a few hundred dollars now and then. I thought it was okay to live from pay check to pay check. I couldn't afford credit cards, but wasn't able to live without them either. My credit report got to be horrible. I had to resort to getting loans, and borrowing money from friends and family.

You would see me driving older cars, and if anything went wrong with them, I couldn't afford to fix them or buy another one.

Financial bondage became another source of anger. I got so mad at being so broke. Plus, I was so absorbed with my finances, I wasn't focused on helping people.

I am learning that what I allow my mind to dwell on controls all of my choices, good or bad. I can choose to think angry and codependent thoughts. I can decide to be negative, depressed, and think lowly of myself. I can desire to think of myself as being a victim. However, I can also choose to think positive, happy, and victorious thoughts.

Thus ends my discussion of specific hurts and mindsets that have limited my life. But before I close, I would like to share with you my observations and what I have learned regarding two areas that concern family life, because what I have been through has contributed to much family conflict.

The first area is that of dysfunctional families. Much of what we have discussed can lead to this. I want to list three characteristics. One, there is emotional or physical abuse. Two, there is an inability to communicate or carry on positive, constructive conversations. Three, parents cannot get along, and the children are exposed to the parents' emotional baggage, so the children feel a need to take care of their parents.

The second factor is boundaries. I had never heard of boundaries, as it pertains to families, until I started counselling. Plus, due to my low self-esteem, I never had them. I believe this subject is so important and has been so beneficial to me that I would like to share some thoughts with you.

Let's use the example of having a yard with a fence around it. That is my boundary. Inside that fence are things with which I identify. They are mine. Hopefully, I take pride in them and do not allow others to mess them up or destroy them. I do not permit my neighbors to dump their trash in my yard.

Okay, now put this example on the emotional level. There are defining characteristics that make me who I am, and that have a bearing upon how happy I am as an individual. I also have moral standards and want to be treated with respect. When other people want me to be someone I am not or want me to do things that decrease my level of happiness, they are up against my boundary line. If others want me to compromise my moral or religious beliefs, they are testing my boundary. Sometimes, people want to dump their emotional garbage on me. Or want me to take on their problems.

In each of these cases, I have a choice. I can allow people to violate my boundary, or I can say, "No." As a substitute teacher, sometimes I refuse to take a particular assignment because I know from past experience that the students are disrespectful, rude, and obnoxious. Now, I can deal with those students appropriately, but I also do not need to put myself in that kind of situation if not necessary.

My health and safety is also a boundary. Maintaining a positive attitude is a boundary. If possible, I need to pull myself out of environments that are not conducive to maintaining good health, safety, and a positive attitude.

In short, I do not have to put up with &%$#* in my life. I have learned that it is not selfish to want to take care of myself. I have needs that require nurturing. When I had really low self-esteem, I allowed unwanted things to come into my life and then got angry because of it. As I already mentioned, I used to not have any boundaries, not only because of low self-esteem, but also because of the belief that the more accepting and tolerant I was of people and circumstances, the more spiritual I was.

As I said at the beginning, I am certainly no expert in any area discussed in this chapter, but I have simply spoken from personal experience. What is significant is that I have begun to change from a belief system that limited me to one that is beginning to liberate me, to truly live life as God intended because I have seen the need for it, and consequently, have become open to growth and change.

If you are having trouble in any of these areas or others not mentioned, please consider getting help. You do not have to go through life accepting less than what you want, or allowing circumstances or people to hold you back. Generally, you will not hear sermons in church about these things, or even hear Christians talk about them.

Happiness is a choice. You can start experiencing victory. You can begin to mature as a Christian. You can embark upon a journey of moving ahead for God. The road to recovery is never too late.

Chapter 8

THE ROAD TO RECOVERY: IT'S NEVER TOO LATE

Behind Every Dark Shadow Is A Light Somewhere

Recovery began with recognizing that there was a problem. It is called coming out of denial. It is owning the problem and taking responsibility for it. I realized that certain parts of my life had become unmanageable, and that I had a tendency to do the wrong thing.

Why do many Christians not recognize nor want to admit that they have problems in need of recovery? I believe there are several reasons, most of which were true of me.

- They think that Christians are not supposed to have certain types of problems, so by admitting to them, it may cause them to question their salvation.
- They fear being judged or thought less of by others.
- Some problems are so subtle they may not be recognized as being problems, for example, thinking incorrectly about oneself, God, or others.
- They think that they might be disqualified for leadership positions in the Church. (Depending upon the type of problem or the religious denominations, this could be true in some cases.)
- They view a problem in their life as not being a big deal.
- They find a way to justify the problem instead of assuming responsibility for it.

- They want to be seen as a role model and good example to their family and church.
- If people really knew what they are like, they might lose their "following," and the finances that go with it.

As a Christian, it is a recognition that only by God's power and grace is recovery possible. It still requires a huge amount of conscious, disciplined effort. As important as prayer and Bible reading are, recovery for me required using many other "tools" that God has provided.

Before I started recovery, I had all the aforementioned problems, but did not know even where to begin. In addition, I had no idea what the causes were or how to overcome them, but I was ready to do whatever worked within biblical boundaries to solve them including secular methods and sources. I began asking the question, "Why am I living a life of defeat and mediocrity, and many other people are so positive and accomplishing great things for God, even to the point of having worldwide ministries?" To seek an answer to this question, I began reading books.

Reading

The first book I read was *My Journey: From an Iowa Farm to a Cathedral of Dreams*, by Robert Schuller, of the Hour of Power. This is his autobiography and the story behind the building of the Crystal Cathedral and his worldwide ministry. I found the answer to my question in this book. One of the first very obvious things I discovered is that he had a positive goal-oriented mindset even in his childhood.

You see, who we become starts in the way we are programmed even as a child. This is nothing new, but I believe at times we do not realize how serious of a problem it can be. We rise to the level of our own thinking and expectations. We will never achieve more than for which we are willing to settle.

There are many Christians like Robert Schuller, but his book was the one I "happened" to read, through God's providence. I realized right then and there that I needed to completely reprogram my thinking. God has used and continues to use books in a miraculous way. I embarked upon going to the library on a regular basis to check out books. I could not stop reading! I was reading three to four books a month. It was helping me with my problems by transforming my thinking. When I checked out another book, it would continue right where the former one left off. I believe the Holy Spirit was directing me in choosing books. I had a part-time job for awhile working as a custodian and what kind of building was I cleaning? Of all places, a library! As I was cleaning, I would see a book I wanted to check out and would go back the next day and get it. God's grace and sovereignty is so good!

I have gone on to read over 200 books. I read positive thinking books, motivational books, autobiographies about people who have overcome horrible obstacles and setbacks, books on success principles, and books on self-improvement and making the most of myself. I got my hands on anything and everything that would change my thinking. Little by little, step-by-step, I was becoming less of what I had been, and more of what I desired to be.

My counselor told me later that reading played a major role in bringing me out of depression. Reading and filling my mind with constant positive thoughts produced neurochemicals in my brain. Reading was far more instrumental than I first thought at the time in assisting in my recovery. It contributed to literally saving my life.

Counseling

About the same time that I started reading books, I began seeing a counselor. Counseling started to dissect my past, way back to my earliest years, to bring to the surface the root causes of why I was like I was. That is when I first recognized that my life had been controlled to a very large extent by anger and low self-esteem, and compounded by many other related problems. I began to understand myself for the very first time at the age of 51! Counseling was the beginning of what would be a very long, pain-stakingly slow and gruelling process or recovery. There is a saying that goes,

"Time is a healer of hurts." In my case, it would take time and a whole lot of discipline, conscious effort, and hard work. It would not be easy, but it had to be done. It was not an option.

I grew up believing that Christians should not have to go to counseling. Bible reading, prayer, and "walking with God," I was told, could solve all of my problems. The "daily quiet time" was stressed. These were all, of course, very important, but with me they were not automatic cure-alls for my problems. I had mindsets and habits that had become so engrained in my character, that it was going to require counseling to break the strongholds of the past. Does this mean that the Word of God and prayer are not strong enough to do so? Let me leave that question hanging and I will get back to it.

I have heard some pastors say that everything relates to a spiritual condition. If you are a pastor who believes this way, I beg to differ with you. Here's why. For example, is being a *victim* of physical or emotional abuse a spiritual problem? Does a child who has been called stupid, or told that he will never amount to anything, have a spiritual problem? Fortunately, I never had those labels placed upon me at home or at school, but many people have. Is the inability of a husband or wife to communicate a spiritual problem? Not necessarily. It could be not knowing the correct words to speak or body language, using the proper tone of voice with one's mate. I could go on and on. True, failure to turn to the power of God in overcoming problems is a spiritual condition, but the initial cause may not be. The person causing the abuse has a spiritual problem, not the victim. We must distinguish between the two.

When I have gone to talk to someone about problems in my life and have been told that it is simply a spiritual condition, not only was the root cause not dealt with, but I went away with a guilt complex, or started to wonder if my Christian beliefs were relevant. I was not really helped by answers like, "Just trust God" or "God has a reason for this." It is true that in all situations I *should* trust God and He *has* a reason behind it, *but these answers should not be given as a substitute for not knowing how to deal with the circumstances because one is not trained to do so.* If it was possible to make sense and understanding come out of the situation, then that is what I wanted. If there were possible solutions to a problem, then that is what I expected. I did not want religious phrases tossed at me in place of understanding and solutions. It would have been better for me if I had simply been told, "I am not trained to help you, but I can give you some names of people, or support ministries, that can."

When people tried to put "spiritual bandages on my emotional wounds," the bleeding was still there. My hurts were below the surface and so subtle, that they were not recognized on Sunday mornings, and unless I talked about them with someone who was trained, I would not get the help I needed.

I was very good at playing "emotional hide and seek." I had hidden hurts that I knew needed to be healed, but I did not tell anyone. The "Hello, how are you? I'm fine," greeting had become so standard for me, like it has for everyone else. I was not being honest with myself or with others. One time recently, I responded to a person asking me how I was doing, by saying, "Well, that depends upon what area of my life you are talking about." That individual did not know what to say. Sometimes the people we least suspect are the ones who need healing the most.

When people have hurts, they want to talk about healing and may not be ready to discuss how to get to heaven. We need to meet people where they are, not where we want or think them to be. Is it being honest and realistic to believe that someone wants to "wait on the Lord," or "just pray about it," or "just turn it over to Jesus," when, for example, their family doesn't have the food they need because the husband is out of work with no benefits? I do not think so!

A trained counselor may be needed. Granted, such a person costs money. Even through counseling it may take a long time for hurts to heal. God can lead you to the right *Christian* counselor. I found one right in my immediate area, but I had to take the initiative and open up the telephone directory. God used the yellow pages.

How has Christian counseling helped me? One, it has helped me identify the causes of my hurts. Two, it has shown me how my childhood has influenced my adult life. Three, I have begun to see how problems have common elements. Four, many of my problems are behavior patterns that can be changed. Five, there has been discussion relating to how religious upbringing can cause problems later in life. Six, it has provided emotional support with comfort, but sometimes with the stark reality of what I need to change. Seven, it has helped me to recognize that there is a mind-body connection. These are all areas which may require counseling.

To get a little more specific in my case, it has been brought to my attention through counseling that my past has included emotional abuse, (at school, like I mentioned earlier in the locker room in junior high school), negative mindsets, repressed emotions, and unresolved issues.

Counseling has helped guide me through the healing process, which has proven to be very valuable in understanding myself and helping other people heal as well. I believe that the healing process has an advantage over instantaneous, divine deliverances. It is personal growth and an ability to relate to other people who are going through the same struggles.

Another way I have been helped is in the family context. I came to the realization of how much emotional baggage I brought into my marriage. That could be a topic for another book.

Now I will answer the question posed at the beginning of this section. The Word of God is strong enough, along with prayer, to break the barriers of our past, IF we interpret it properly, apply it correctly, and do what it says.

I would like to contrast three verses of Scripture to give biblical support to the preceding paragraph. The first one, mentioned earlier, is II Timothy 2:15. "Be diligent to present yourself approved to God as a workman who does not need to be ashamed, handling accurately the Word of truth." Coupled with this is II Timothy 3:16. "All Scripture is inspired by God, and profitable for teaching, for reproof, for correction, for training in righteousness." In contrast to these, however, is II Peter 3:16. "… the untaught and unstable distort, as they do also the rest of the Scriptures, to their own destruction." So, if Scripture is not interpreted and applied properly, it can destroy us instead of empowering us.

The problem is that we can allow the power of the Scriptures to be short circuited in several ways. According to Matthew 13:19-22 there are five reasons listed as to why the word of God may not take effect in one's life: 1) It is not understood, 2) the hearer has no firm root in himself, 3) worry, 4) deceitfulness of riches, and 5) tradition (which, I believe, could include one's belief system.)

Remember, too, that the Bible is a book of principles, and sometimes, but not always, a detailed road map that tells us a step-by-step process to get from a point A to point B. That is where, I believe, counseling and other "tools" God has given us come into play.

Some pastors are trained counselors. If so, fine. If not, the pastor can be a good listener, but there is no way he can be of help to you in all of the areas that enter into healing your hurts. I am not trying to be critical of pastors! I am simply saying they are pastors, not professional counsellors. The bottom line is to get the help you need. If you do not, it will end up being much more costly in broken relationships, unhappiness, and being held back in life. If you are a Christian, you can be so much more effective for God, experience victory and maturity, and move ahead, when you deal with barriers in your life. I encourage you to get help.

There is another option that does not cost anything. It may not give you all the help that you need, but it would give you some wisdom and guidance. You may consider joining some kind of support group or recovery ministry through a local church. Hopefully, as you are reading this, you are at the point in your life where you recognize that you need help. I got to the point where I had to swallow my pride and attitude of self-sufficiency, and learn to say three words: I need help!

The following section was written by the professional counselor I went to for several years.

The author honored me with the request that I offer my insights regarding Christian counseling. It is with humbleness, and my profound understanding of my faithful call to God's grace, that I do so. What I have to share, is not the final word on the subject of counseling from the Christian perspective. However, it is my prayer that what I share from my personal and ongoing struggle with God's grace and will, might be of help to at least one of God's other children.

The aim of the therapy offered by myself has less to do with "advice," but more to do with the struggle to "be" with my clients as they choose the options that best fit their situations within their own cultural perspectives.

In my experience, people come for therapy/counseling with problems, dilemmas, quandaries, pain, grief, and confusion. Occasionally, they wish to explore the reasons and direction in which their lives have gone or are going. Then, they can choose their direction/adjustment for the future. In the agency within which I practice (Christian Counseling Service), the "plan of action" depends upon counselor/client joint option-choices and trust, counselor supervision, and timely reviews.

Some of the gravest stumbling blocks to successful conversation can be the "assumptions," "preconceptions," and "perspectives" that each person brings. These possible blocks come from our cultural, societal, religious, educational, plus family experiences and values. They influence every conversation that we have, including the ones that are named "fights," "arguments," "debates," "mental, emotional, physical and verbal abuses," plus "advice," "Bible studies," "prayer chains," and "sermons."

"Advice" usually makes me think of "vice," as it so frequently is meant. It comes from those trying to be helpful, gossipers, the

mean spirited, plus the plethora of "how-to/self-help" books and all other media.

Therefore, it is essential that a client/counselor relationship begin with examining each possible stumbling block for what it is and choosing the concept of "discernment" to be followed. (When used as a noun, discernment means the trait of judging wisely and objectively; knowing; perception.)

Sharon (Carlson) Graham-Laraene is a practicing Christian counselor. She has a Masters of Social Work, a Bachelor of Social Anthropology, and is an ordained minister of the United Methodist Church.

Christian Television

God used Christian television broadcasts in the same way He used books. There were several positive-minded, uplifting pastors who emphasized healing that were ministering to me. Every time I tuned into one of them, even for a few minutes, they were speaking about something that I needed to hear right at that time. It was always something that added little by little, to my recovery. Again, it was not a coincidence! God had a plan to bring me out of my past and to transform my thinking by getting rid of the negative, mental strongholds that had held me back for nearly all of my life.

Keeping A Journal

I was hearing and reading so many sayings that were impacting my life, I decided I wanted to begin writing them down, so I initiated a journal. Included also in the journal were good things that were happening.

Journaling is a tool for healing because it helps a person focus on God's grace. It assists in maintaining a positive attitude. As acts of the goodness of God are written down, it is an instrument for seeing "bright spots" in life. A person can thumb through the journal from time to time and reflect on how much growth has taken place. This adds encouragement and hope to the recovery process.

The more I dwell on the positive, the more it drowns out the negative. Proverbs 23:7 says, "For as he thinks within himself, so he is…" The key work here is *thinks*. That can also mean "*dwell on*." Being positive helps me control my anger and codependent reactions.

Some sayings from my journal have helped keep me particularly focused:

1. Always assume the positive.
2. My best is yet to come.
3. I refuse to worry about things beyond my control.
4. Grace is being accepted before I become acceptable.
5. Turn anger into positive action.
6. It's always too soon to quit.
7. Grow so that I might glow.
8. Choose to do what makes me happy
9. God will always have the last word.
10. God has no problems, only plans.

By the same token, I have developed some thoughts in my journal concerning the grace of God:

1. God can take me from being barren to being beautiful.
2. If it wasn't for God's grace I could not acknowledge the full truth about myself.
3. I grow better in sunshine and love, and the light of His Holy Spirit to impel choices to see positive change.
4. God will go out of His way to reach those who are going astray.
5. God leads people to Himself through gentleness, in the midst of adversity.
6. God's grace is instructional, to change us.
7. The more thankful I am; the more grace I will receive.
8. God sees beyond my faults to my needs.

Scripture Memorization

Memorizing Scripture is, I believe, the best way I have found to bring every thought captive to the obedience of Christ. It helps keep my thinking in check. It helps insure that I am thinking correct thoughts toward God, others, and myself. I try to be selective in memorizing Scripture verses that zero in on my particular needs, and I write them on 3 by 5 cards.

I would like to share with you a system that makes memorization fun. I take the verses I have written on 3 by 5 cards and keep them in my car or my pocket. When I have what I call "mental down time," like waiting to pick up someone, waiting for a train to cross, or waiting for an appointment, I flip through my cards.

One of the passages which has helped me the most is Philippians 4:4-8. "*Rejoice in the Lord always; again, I say rejoice! Let your forebearing spirit be known to all men. The Lord is near. Be anxious for nothing, but in everything by prayer and supplication with thanksgiving, let your requests be made known to God. And the peace of God, which surpasses all comprehension, shall guard your hearts and your minds in Christ Jesus. Finally, brethren, whatever is true, whatever is honorable, whatever is right, whatever is pure, whatever is lovely, whatever is of good repute. If there is any excellence and if anything worthy of praise, let your mind dwell on these things.*"

Before I leave the subject of Scripture memory, I would like to share with you some of the verses I am using to help me with my recovery.

1. "*But in all these things we overwhelmingly conquer through Him who loved us.*" (Romans 8:37)
2. "*...Greater is He who is in you, than he who is in the world.*" (I John 4:4)
3. "*Finally, be strong in the Lord, and in the strength of His might.*" (Ephesians 6:10)
4. "*...Fix your hope completely on the grace to be brought to you...*" (I Peter 1:13)

5. "*What shall we say then? Are we to continue in sin that grace might increase*?" (Romans 6:1)
6. "*There is therefore now no condemnation for those who are in Christ Jesus*." (Romans 8:1)
7. "*Seek the Lord while He may be found; call upon Him while He is near. Let the wicked forsake his way, and the unrighteous man his thoughts, and let him return to the Lord, and He will have compassion on him, and to our God, for He will abundantly pardon*." (Isaiah 55:6-7)

From these passage, it can clearly be seen that recovery involves the power of God, the grace of God, and a change in one's thinking and behavior. These verses also teach that there is no condemnation on the part of God toward whatever it is that a person may be going through. The realization that God did not look down on me because of my struggles, was a huge step in my recovery. It played a big part in changing me.

These are beautiful verses to claim in seeing deliverance. There are many others that you will find as you study Scripture, because God is in the business of restoring people's lives, and restoring people to Himself. I have listed some verses in the back of the book, in Appendix 1.

To make Scripture memory even more powerful, personalize the verses by inserting the pronouns, "me" and "I" where appropriate. An example is, "But in all these things (I) overwhelmingly conquer through Him who loves (me)."

I will conclude by simply saying that, for me, Scripture memory is not an option, it is a necessity!

Positive Affirmation and the Power of Our Words

I have used a lot of positive affirmations. Positive affirmations are statements I say or think concerning the kind of person I want to become, or where I want to go with my life. Words can be "tools" to bring about change. I use them whenever necessary to refocus or reinforce my thinking. These statements are in the present tense. The brain believes everything it is told, whether it is good or bad, positive or negative, truth or lie. That is why it is so important to feed our minds with thoughts and words that are good, positive, and true. When this is combined with personalizing Scripture verses, it is a powerful combination. Here are some examples of positive affirmations, some using Scripture:

1. I choose to be happy.
2. I am expecting great things to happen today.
3. I am a person of worth and value.
4. I am positively influencing the lives of others.
5. All people have value in God's eyes, and because of this, even with their needs and hurts, they are worthy of my attention.
6. This week I am practicing rejoicing, thankfulness, and praying without ceasing. (I Thess. 5:16)
7. I think highly of others, and give preference to them in honor. (Romans 12:10)
8. I do small acts of kindness.
9. I listen intently, without interrupting, to the words and emotions of others.
10. I build up people in front of others.

In my life I have had the enemies of low self-esteem, anger, being negative, and all of the other things I have talked about. Positive affirmations and Scripture memory have helped counteract these enemies by causing the opposite trait to become embedded in my mind. Sometime this may require force-feeding when a person doesn't feel like thinking positively; make yourself say these things.

Let me take this one step further. The way one talks, and the words that are used, especially claiming God's promises out loud over the problems in the name of Jesus, can activate His angels, reverse curses, and cause Satan to flee. As believers, we have the authority to do this.

Visualization

Remember, I stated in chapter 5, that visualization changed me as a teacher. It can work in any area of life. Let's review what it is. Visualization is forming mental images. It is seeing in your mind's eye how you want to be, or where you want to go in life. It gives an additional boost to something becoming part of one's subconscious. Several examples as to how I use this technique may be helpful:

1. If I get upset and react to a person or a situation, I can visualize how I could have responded in a controlled and patient manner. I review with mental pictures the situation, and then picture myself responding in a positive way.
2. I visualize myself going up to a person, looking them in the eyes, calling them by name, and giving them a firm handshake.
3. When I go to the library, I visualize seeing this very book on the shelf, with the title and my name on it.

If anyone takes issue with this technique, saying it is human effort and not relying upon God, my answer is, first of all, it works. Second, I believe it is taking advantage of the potential of our brain with which God created us, to bring about positive change. Third, I see nothing wrong with applying so-called "secular techniques" to bring spiritual growth and maturity.

The Role of the Local Church

I want to shift attention to local churches. There is a big difference in churches. I am not talking about size of congregation, style of music, or forms of worship. What I am referring to are attitudes toward people with problems and needs. Is there an acceptance of people who are "different" from the typical Sunday morning worshipper? Attitudes within churches can either get them out of their comfort zone or hold them back from ministering. Some churches that I have been in have *judged* the sinner instead of showing how to be *justified* in Christ. Some churches are shocked and unaccepting of someone when they disclose a hidden hurt or sin.

There are other attitudes that can move people forward or stifle their growth. Some churches lay a guilt trip on people because they are not doing what others think they should be doing. In addition, others are bound by tradition. On the other hand, there are churches that are very positive and open minded in helping people where they hurt. Included in this category are churches that are accepting of all cultures, even to the point of being interracial. Being in a church that supports you in your recovery is critical.

Is the church you attend helping or hindering your growth? Are you *growing or just going*? Do you go just because it is the thing to do, or because you really look forward to going? I truly believe a person can be excited about attending church. If you are not, perhaps a change is in order.

In the words of my former counselor, "Church should be biblical, relevant and, in the case of children and youth, FUN!"

The local church plays a vital role in how we grow or don't grow. Find a church that will help you recover. Get out of a church that judges you and makes you feel guilty or think less of yourself. Some churches have small support groups for people with problems. I am presently involved in one, and it is contributing to my recovery and giving me opportunities to minister to others.

As Christians, we all have a responsibility to support one another. Galatians 6:1-2 says, "*Brethren, even if a man is caught in any trespass, you who are spiritual, restore such a one in a spirit of gentleness; each one looking to yourself, lest you too be tempted. Bear one another's burdens, and thus fulfill the law of Christ.*" The local church should be a safe haven for sharing our hurts and experiencing healing.

For this to happen, however, we must be open and honest with one another. As I mentioned in a previous chapter, the word, "Fine," has become such a standard response to the question, "How are you?" This answer really says absolutely nothing about how a person is doing.

What would happen if, the next time someone asks you how you are doing, you responded with one of the following answers:

1. Do you really want to know?
2. Not fine, how are you?
3. Ask my wife, or husband.
4. Actually, I could use some help at the moment.
5. Do you have a moment to talk?
6. Things could be better.
7. It depends upon what area of my life you are talking about.
8. Fantastic!
9. It's a fabulous day!
10. I'm basking in God's blessings.

Try these if you dare, and see how they work on people. They will probably turn a few heads and raise a few eyebrows, but they will be honest answers that may initiate some profitable conversations, and would disclose our hidden hurts. If they don't, you have nothing to lose. When people tell me to, "Have a nice day," another standard greeting, I am starting to say, "I intend to and want to help others do the same."

Because I really wanted to find understanding and solutions to my struggles, God orchestrated events in my life to bring answers. The counseling, the books, and the new church were not a coincidence. It was and is part of God's plan for me. Jeremiah 29:11 has the encouraging words: "*For I know the plans that I have for you, declares the Lord, plans for welfare and not for calamity to give you a future and a hope*." I am seeing His plan to heal my past unfold before my eyes, and it is exciting (but still difficult). He also has a plan for you. What God has used in my life may be different for you. *A person is never too old to see change unfold*! Whatever may be your struggle, it is not unique to you, and you don't have to go through it alone. If you truly want to change, God will use anything at His disposal, man-made or supernatural, to bring about that change.

The catch is that we must cooperate with His plan. I have used many "methods" to recover. However, if I had been closed minded to so-called secular ways or to switching churches, especially one of a different denomination, I do not believe that I would be very far along in my recovery. Furthermore, if I had slammed the door on counseling, my growth would have been stymied.

Everything, however, hinges upon God's grace, and according to Hebrews 12:15, a bitter and unforgiving spirit can stand in the way:

"*See to it that no one comes short of the grace of God; that no root of bitterness springing up causes trouble, and by it many be defiled.*" This verse clearly teaches that getting rid of bitterness is a prerequisite to experiencing all of God's grace.

All of the things mentioned in this chapter have contributed to my recovery. I have come out of depression and low self-esteem. I no longer have a victim/failure mentality and a negative attitude. I would like to show you how recovery has helped me in these specific areas: anger, codependency, and low self-esteem.

Dealing with Anger

One of the first things I learned was that anger can become a habit and pattern of behavior. I had become accustomed to reacting to another person or situation. After months of discussing causes behind my anger, attention was given to solutions. My recovery from anger consists of the following choices:

1. I have to own the problem. "Blowing up" or yelling is never justified and accomplishes nothing.
2. I need to recognize what sorts of things or situation make me angry.
3. When I know in advance that I might have a situation that has the potential to make me *react*, I can plan in advance how I can *respond* in a non-destructive way.
4. I think of positive alternatives to dealing with the anger, like going for a walk, or going outside and working in the yard. Sometimes I may have to plan what I am going to say.
5. It is important that I vent my anger, and do something to release it, but not around other people.

There are three objectives that I choose to focus on in getting control of anger. One, it is necessary to deal with it so it does not become repressed. Two, it is crucial that the family is not exposed to my emotional outbursts. Three, attempts should be made to keep relationships intact. I have unfortunately discovered that one negative expression of anger directed at a person, even just using the wrong tone of voice, can destroy a relationship. Remember, I have not arrived. I am constantly working on these things, and get lax many times, but it is a strategy to overcome anger.

This can be a good example for our children. It can teach them that it is essential to express themselves and not hold things in. From this they can learn to do it in ways that will not undermine relationships, and expose others to their emotional baggage.

Counteracting Codependency

Every so often, as a result of reading and counseling, I would have "light bulbs" go off in my mind. I would understand something we had been talking about for months. One case was codependency. I made a decision one day that I was not going to allow myself to be controlled by the feelings and reactions of other people. The counselor said it was a big victory! Does that mean I no longer am codependent? No way! I had a realization of what I needed to change, but have a long way to go in doing so. It was, however, a big step in the right direction.

There are several things I am seeking to do in recovering from codependency. One, I am trying to understand the causes. Two, I attempt to stay positive and focused, with an attitude of gratitude. Three, I do not want to dwell on angry thoughts, especially about others. Four, I am learning to set boundaries.

In terms of how I respond to other people, I am seeking to apply the following actions that help me when there is the potential to react in a codependent manner:

1. Lower my tone of voice.
2. Leave the room, go outside and work, or go for a walk.
3. Do some activity to divert my thoughts.

4. Change a potential confrontation into a constructive conversation.
5. Simply refuse to be drawn into a "codependent conversation" or reacting back and forth.
6. Make a decision regardless of the resistance.

Raising My Low Self-Esteem

I would like to share with you ways that have worked for me in raising my low self-esteem:

1. Counseling
2. Reading books on the subject.
3. Force-feeding myself with positive affirmations and self-talk.
4. Setting boundaries.
5. Handling situations and people in a positive way without reacting, so that I feel good about myself.
6. Becoming more other-centered, doing things for people, being a giver.
7. Seeing victory over my destructive habits and mindsets so I no longer see myself as overcome by them, but rather as an overcomer, through God's power and grace.

How To Choose To Be Happy

More and more I am choosing to be happy, and that does not depend upon someone's attitude toward me or my circumstances. Here are some concepts that have worked for me:

1. I refuse to allow others to make me feel responsible for their problems.
2. I am not totally responsible for another person's happiness. There comes a time when a person has to decide that they are going to be happy.
3. I cannot allow myself to expect that I will always meet the expectations of others.
4. I cannot and should not try to change anyone but myself. I can choose to be so focused on becoming all that I can

become and pursuing God-given dreams, that I don't have the mental energy or the time to even think about changing others.

5. I should not allow people to use my behavior as an excuse for them not changing. Just because I have a problem in some area of my life does not mean that someone should use it to justify their problems.
6. I refuse to allow myself to be weighed down by circumstances beyond my control.
7. A big part of choosing to be happy is maintaining a healthy self-image, and taking care of my needs; it is setting boundaries. My needs and desires are important! I have dreams and goals that I need to pursue. I can reward myself by doing fun things.
8. Do the things that make me happy!
9. I must not allow myself to be under the control of other people.

A Disciplined Thought Life

To continue to recover, I must persistently knock down destructive strongholds by "bringing every thought captive to the obedience of Christ." This involves discipline and conscious effort all day long, not just a 30 minute "daily quiet time." So, what needs to happen to accomplish this? I will list what works for me, some of which has already been discussed in this chapter, because for me, recovery is all in how I think.

1. Have an attitude of gratitude and rejoicing. (I Thess. 5:16, Phil 4:4) I can look for the blessings of each day. Sometimes a blessing is something adverse that could happen, but doesn't. Recently there was a severe wind storm in the area where I live. Debris could have flown through the air and damaged my car, but it didn't. That was a blessing. One of the things I sometimes do is to carry a piece of paper in my pocket or in my car, and every time I see a blessing, no matter how small, I write it down. If you are having trouble

seeing "bright spots" in your life, try this method for one week.

No matter what we are going through, if we are not thankful for what we do have, we are not living in God's will, according to I Thess. 5:18. "*In everything give thanks; for this is God's will for you in Christ Jesus.*" When I realized this, it hit me like a ton of bricks, and I determined I had better start having a thankful attitude.

This teaching is reinforced in Romans 5:3-6, which tells us, "*And not only this, but we also exult in our tribulation, knowing that tribulation brings about perseverance; and perseverance, proven character; and proven character, hope; and hope does not disappoint, because the love of God has been poured out within our hearts through the Holy Spirit who was given to us. For while we were still helpless, at the right time Christ died for the ungodly.*"

Along with a thankful attitude is having the sentiment expressed in the Serenity Prayer, the one made famous because of its association with Alcoholics Anonymous, that begins with "God, grant me the serenity to accept the things I cannot change…"

2. Turn problems into prayers. (I Thess. 5:17) "Pray without ceasing." We can always ask God for wisdom and trust His timing and sovereignty. How we pray is important. Remember, earlier, I said I had been praying wrong nearly all of my life. What do I mean by that? There is negative and positive prayer. Let me give you an example: Suppose I am praying that I will get rid of anger. I can pray like this: "O God, you know I have this anger problem. I don't like having anger. Please God, I pray, I really want you to deliver me from anger." The problem is every time we use or think the word "anger," we are reinforcing it in our brain. We become like we think. I suggest to you, would it not be better to pray something like this: "God, I pray, make me into a gentle, loving and caring person who responds to others in a kind

and patient way." When we pray like this our mind is focusing on the kind of person we want to become.

3. Scripture memorization. I talked about this previously and shared with you a method I use.
4. I choose to be positive and happy.
5. I try to think well of other people. (Romans 12:10)
6. I recite positive affirmations.
7. I read books and listen to programs that instill positive thoughts into my brain.
8. I associate with positive-minded people.

I get lax at times, but I try to do some of these things almost every day. At first it was hard to do. Now, by the grace of God and the discipline given by Him, it has become a habit. This simply means I have chosen to develop a routine that keeps me focused in moving in the direction that I want my life to go, by replacing negative habits with positive ones.

Strongholds must not be passed down to the next generation. They must not be permitted to become accepted as normal. Someone in the family needs to decide to break them. That person could be you! They may be generational curses. It is necessary for our children to see that change is possible. They need an example that a person does not have to remain "stuck" in some negative, destructive problem. One of the best things for our children to realize when they leave home is that it is possible to live a life of victory.

A disciplined mind can be summarized in the two Great Commandments, "Love the Lord with all your heart, mind, and soul, and your neighbor as yourself." This is basically telling us that we should think correctly about, and be committed to God, others, and ourselves. Even discipline comes from God, as we are told in II Timothy 1:7 "*For God has not given us a spirit of timidity, but of power, and love and discipline*."

Recovery has not just been dealing with issues, and seeing them continually get better. It has taken discipline to be disciplined! Many times I have relapses. I have reverted back to my old ways. Sometimes I have felt like I was back at the beginning. It has been as though I have not made any progress at all, and I get very discouraged and depressed. There have been days when I have had a really bad attitude, and I didn't even care that I did. Some days at home with the family I have to consciously think about responding, and not reacting, if someone says something that might "set me off," or to not say something that may make someone else angry.

Many times I have thought I am making good progress in a particular area, and then I say or do something (or don't do something) that I considered a major setback. I have thought, "What is the point of it all?" If the people closest to me don't notice a change, then I guess I am not changing. But I was changing in such little ways, so gradually, that it wasn't noticeable to people who were around me every day.

When I went to visit my parents in San Diego, whom I had not seen in several years, my mom remarked that I sure had changed. That was a real boost for me. Other people who have not been around me for some time have said the same thing.

Applying the concepts and "behavior patterns of change" learned in recovery has not been easy. It has been downright tough, to say the least! Recovery is not just for those who have experienced victory. It is for those who have taken responsibility for their problems and have decided to do something about them, with the realization that they are powerless to overcome them on their own strength. Every day, with the help of other people and the "strategies" mentioned in this chapter, combined with God's grace, I have to work at conquering myself. Even after many years of recovery, I am still at times dealing with the same issues with which I started. I can be my own worst enemy. Yet, the Bible says in Romans 8:37 that I am more than a conqueror. Every person can either choose to be overcome by the struggles of life, or choose to be an overcomer by claiming God's promises.

God is always presenting me with opportunities to see positive change in my life. If I combine being goal oriented with an attitude of expecting good things to happen, I will recognize these "providential circumstances." I am learning to make the most of my life, in spite of my struggles.

I am being liberated from mindsets of the past. In some ways I feel like I was a caterpillar inside the cocoon of my own negative, limiting, destructive belief system, but now I am in the process of breaking out and becoming a beautiful, free butterfly. My low self-esteem is rising. I am able to take criticism. Compliments are well received. I engage in conversations more with others, because I know I have something to offer them. Things are not done anymore just to gain recognition. I am breaking free from the bondage of a distorted view of God's will, and a lack of success orientation. I am being liberated from the bondage of other people, being myself more and not trying to live according to the expectations of others.

I no longer allow people to walk all over me. Being spiritual does not mean that I have to be a doormat, or accept whatever comes. I confront situations and deal with them promptly, so they don't fester within me for months. When I say, "confront," I do not mean I become hostile and destroy relationships, but I speak up. I do not pretend that some situation is just going to go away, and I do not intend to allow it to lower my self-esteem. It may not always have a positive outcome, but at least I know that I dealt with it. How I handle my circumstances in general and specific situations and issues in my life do play a role in my recovery. There are still times, of course, when I do not handle situations well and consequently think poorly of myself, but these are becoming less and less.

Hang in there! At some point in time, if you really want to change and are seeking God's help, believe that God will deliver you out of your situation in which you may feel stuck or is beyond your control. Let's look at the story in John 5:1-9.

"After these things there was a feast of the Jews, and Jesus went up to Jerusalem. Now there is in Jerusalem by the sheep gate a pool, which is called in Hebrew Bethesda, having five porticoes.

In these lay a multitude of those who were sick, blind, lame, and withered, [waiting for the moving of the waters; for an angel of the Lord went down at certain seasons into the pool, and stirred up the water; whoever then first, after the stirring up of the water, stepped in was made well from whatever disease with which he was afflicted.] And a certain man was there, who had been thirty-eight years in his sickness. When Jesus saw him lying there, and knew that he had already been a long time in that condition, He said to him, 'Do you wish to get well?' The sick man answered him, 'Sir, I have no man to put me into the pool when the water is stirred up, but while I am coming, another steps down before me.' Jesus said to him, 'Arise, take up your pallet, and walk.' And immediately the man became well, and took up his pallet and began to walk."

While you are waiting for God to change your circumstances, seek His presence and the power of the Holy Spirit. Scripture tells us that He is our comforter, instructor, helper, and giver of joy and peace.

Sometimes, however, we just have to say, "*Thy will be done.*"

INTRODUCTION TO CHAPTERS 9, 10, 11

No matter what your circumstances you might be encouraged to know that you can move ahead with your life and go places where you have never imagined. I never dreamed six years ago that I would be writing a book.

The next three chapters talk about success, developing your potential, and being fashioned for a fruitful life as a Christian. After reading these chapters, it is my hope and prayer that you will see yourself as God sees you: forgiven and useful to Him. He loves you so much that He doesn't look at you according to your past, but in view of your potential.

If you truly desire to rise above where you are right now and make the most of your life for God's glory, then these chapters are for you. It will take a steady diet of reprogrammed thinking to do so, but by God' grace, it can happen.

How many Christians do you know who talk about principles of success and motivation around other Christians or at church? The answer is probably none. It is a subject that typically is reserved for the business world. As I mentioned in a previous chapter, it also is a topic from which Christians have a tendency to shy away because, for many of them, as it used to be in my case, it is not spiritual or shows a lack of surrender to God. Nothing could be further from the truth.

God wants us to be success oriented, but it is how success is defined that makes the difference as to whether or not it glorifies God. If you are one of those Christians who believe, as I did, that Christians are not supposed to strive to be successful, then hopefully you will be challenged to rise to a new level in your thinking.

Chapter 9

SCRIPTURE AND SUCCESS

The Bible is God's Success Manual

As I have already mentioned, I used to not be able to blend spirituality and success. I know now that one does not necessarily contradict the other. There are many successful, Christian businessmen and women. God wants me to become all that I can for Him, and to maximize my effectiveness in the lives of others.

What do I mean when I speak of success? First of all, I am *not* saying that Christians should seek to be wealthy, however, there is nothing wrong with wealth as long as it is not used for selfish gain and purposes.

Let's focus again, for a moment, on the money aspect of success. I believed for a long time that Christians should not aspire to make a lot of money. An often-quoted verse was, "*For the love of money is a root of all sorts of evil...*" (I Timothy 6:10) This verse is another one that has been misunderstood. People have used it in my life to support the teaching that it is wrong to make a lot of money. Notice the preceding context in verses 6-8. "*But godliness actually is a means of great gain, when accompanied by contentment. For we have brought nothing into the world, so we cannot take anything out of it either. And if we have food and covering, with these we shall be content.*" It talks about godliness and contentment. Therefore, this verse is saying that when someone loves making money without these two elements, then it is wrong. This misunderstanding contributed to my limiting and confusing beliefs.

Success is not just about money. Money is simply a unit of exchange. Some people have more than others. Success is a journey of continually developing one's potential, refusing to quit, and positively influencing the lives of other people along the way. A person like myself, therefore, can be considered successful even though I have very little money.

I *am* saying that Christians would find it beneficial to think success (as opposed to failure) in everything that is done. This includes thinking positively about oneself and life in general. We can choose to be goal oriented and focused. We can choose to consistently plow ahead in the pursuit of goals, and in becoming our best self. A person does not have to compromise his spirituality or God's will to do this.

A basic principle of success is to never, never quit. It means to pursue your dreams, and let nothing stop you. I would love to have the freedom to do whatever I really want, without money being a restriction. It would not surprise me if a lot of Christians feel the same way, but they are bound by a belief system that is not necessarily biblical, like I was, that holds them back.

In my opinion, as a result of being around Christians all of my life, I believe that a lot of them have shied away from having a success mindset because they have been told, or somehow have gotten the idea that to do so is an indication of lack of surrender to God and His will. Success has been thought of only in terms of how the world defines it: money, nice things, a life style of self-sufficiency, and luxury. Along side this, many Christians probably do not have a clearly defined focus as to what constitutes success.

In the book, *Success, Motivation, and the Scripture*, by William H. Cook, the author has this to say:

"*Proponents of success and proponents of the spiritual life have fought to a standoff. On the one hand, there is the success-bug who has never figured out how to maintain his success-image and still be spiritual. So he concludes, wrongfully, that his is the only team really in the ball game. On the other end of the field is the individual who views his relationship with God as being of prime importance. He is suspicious of accepting new ideas about success and motivation until he is sure they do not rob him of what he already has. So the life of maximum achievement God intended never seems to bounce in his direction."*[2.]

In my view, one needs to be constantly moving forward on God-given goals, while at the same time, be waiting on God to cause everything to come together. A saying I recently saw on a church sign read, "Patience is trusting God's timing." Waiting on God means His timing is perfect. Christians can have confidence that He will put us in the right place, at the proper time, with the right people and resources, to accomplish His objectives.

What does the Bible say about success? Plenty! In this chapter, I will discuss success from some different angles. Comparisons will be made between self-help books and several passages of Scripture. In addition, I will show that success has many other elements besides money. From the many books that I have read on success, I have learned that many people, who have become successful in terms of having a lot of money, have not made money a goal, but rather money came as a result. I will conclude the chapter by giving my definition of success from a Christian perspective.

Let's turn our attention first to self-help books. People have often criticized them, saying they do not line up with Scripture. That is true in some cases, but not all. As the saying goes, "Don't throw out the baby with the bath water." About one third of all of the books that I have read have dealt with success. I have found much useful material that *does* agree with Scripture.

Why then is there an apparent wide rift between self-help books and the Bible? On one hand there is the misunderstanding of Scripture by well-meaning believers. To use one example, one prominent author and pastor made a statement in a book that said

---

2. William H. Cook. *Success, Motivation, and the Scripture.* (Nashville: Broadman Press, 1974) Introductory page. Copyright 1974, Broadman Press. All rights reserved. Used by permission.

goal setting is man-centered. My response to that is that it can be, but not necessarily. It depends upon the attitude of the heart. Does this statement mean that once we become Christians and focused on God and the spiritual surrender of our lives, that we are to no longer set goals? I cringe at the thought! Then we wind up with a whole lot of goal-less Christians who are accomplishing nothing for God. I find no place in Scripture that says that having goals is man-centered. I believe that this thinking is possibly an over-reaction to the lack of spiritual surrender. By God's grace, we have some believers in this generation who have goals that are God-centered with the end result of bringing glory to Him. As a result we have the Crystal Cathedral, Liberty University, CBN Television and the *Left Behind* series, to name several examples.

Yet, in contrast to all of this, we find godless, self-centered individuals. This creates a lot of confusion, and widens the gap between what some self-help books teach, and what some people *think* the Bible says. Furthermore, there are two other well-known extremes. One teaching that some people preach is to stay broke and trust God. The other is prosperity theology. In my view, I do not believe that either one is biblical.

Several factors support my belief that the gap between success books and the Bible is not as wide as many think. One, Scripture must be properly understood. Two, many success principles are right out of the Bible, even though many non-Christians do not realize it. Three, not all godless, non-Christians are greedy and self-serving.

I will take several well-known passages of Scripture and compare them to principles I have read in many success books. When this is done, not only will there be a similarity, but also it will be seen that it is possible to follow success principles with the intention of fulfilling God's purpose and improving our spiritual walk. In my book, that is a winning God-honoring combination. Here we go!

The first passage is Philippians 3:12-14. In these verses we read:

"Not that I have already obtained it, or have already become perfect, but I press on in order that I may lay hold of that for which also I was laid hold of by Christ Jesus. Brethren, I do not regard myself as having laid hold of it yet; but one thing I do: forgetting what lies behind and reaching forward to what lies ahead. I press on toward the goal for the prize of the upward call of God in Christ Jesus."

1. "I press on," means to continually move ahead with persistence.
2. "This one thing I do" can be another way of saying, "Be focused."
3. "Forgetting what lies behind" can mean to get over your past.
4. "Reaching forward to what lies ahead" is like saying to go for it with all you have.
5. "I press on toward the goal" is simply telling us to be goal-oriented.
6. "For the prize of the upward call of God in Christ Jesus" challenges us to go for something bigger than what we are able to accomplish without God's power.

The next passage is I Timothy 4:15-16. The context of this section talks about, beginning in verse 12, speech, conduct, love, faith, purity, public reading of Scripture, exhortation, teaching and one's spiritual gifts. Now in verses 15-16 it says:

"Take pains with these things; be absorbed in them, so that your progress may be evident to all. Pay close attention to yourself, and to your teaching; persevere in these things; for as you do this you will insure salvation both for yourself and for those who hear you."

1. "Take pains with these things" could include getting out of our comfort zones, being disciplined, and doing whatever is required. Success is spelled WORK.
2. "Be absorbed in them" could be another way of saying, "Have a passion for."
3. "So your progress may be evident to all" is similar to saying that other people will see you are committed to changing.
4. "Pay close attention to yourself" would appear to mean working on changing yourself, take responsibility for your actions and attitudes.
5. "Persevere" means to never, never quit, and overcome the obstacles.

In this passage we see a lot of self-improvement as the central issue. From my experience, I can hear some Christians saying that we are supposed to rely solely upon the Word of God and prayer, and not self-effort, but I believe that it is clear that this passage is talking about self-improvement.

Hebrews 12:1-2 is the next Scripture in which to draw our attention.

"*Therefore, since we have so great a cloud of witnesses, surrounding us, let us also lay aside every encumbrance, and the sin which so easily entangles us, and let us run with endurance the race that is set before us, fixing our eyes on Jesus, the author and perfecter of faith, who for the joy set before Him, endured the cross, despising the shame, and has sat down at the right hand of the throne of God.*"

1. "Lay aside every encumbrance," means to get rid of anything holding us back, and break the strongholds.
2. "Sin which so easily entangles us," means to deal with our habits, hurts, and hang-ups.
3. "Run with endurance" can mean to work hard and never quit.

4. "Endured the cross," from a spiritual standpoint, means to sacrifice.
5. "Sat down at the right hand of the throne of God," meant that for Christ, His sacrifice resulted in greater blessing. There is application here to our lives, to have a vision for something greater than the sacrifice.

Our next passage to consider is James 4:13-15.

"*Come now, you who say, 'Today or tomorrow, we shall go to such and such a city, and spend a year there and engage in business and make a profit.' Yet you do not know what your life will be like tomorrow. You are just a vapor that appears for a little while and then vanishes away. Instead you ought to say, "If the Lord wills, we shall live and also do this or that'.*"

1. "Today, or tomorrow, we shall go to such and such a city" refers to having a plan.
2. "Spend a year there and engage in business and make profit" talks about setting a goal and a time frame in which to accomplish your goals.
3. "You do not know what your life will be like tomorrow," means to never discount the uncertainties of life. There are some things beyond our control. Accept what cannot be changed.
4. "If the Lord wills, we shall live and also do this or that" means to always acknowledge and be submissive to God's will; He may have other plans.

This passage admonishes us to never leave God out of our plans, and that events may not go according to our plans. Notice, this passage does *not* say that we should not have goals.

The last passage I would like for us to look at is II Timothy 2:1-6.

"*You therefore, my son, be strong in the grace that is in Christ Jesus. And the things which you have heard from me in the pres-*

ence of many witnesses, these entrust to faithful men, who will be able to teach others also. Suffer hardship with me, as a good soldier of Christ Jesus. No soldier in active service entangles himself in the affairs of everyday life, so that he may please the one who enlisted him as a soldier. And also if anyone competes as an athlete, he does not win the prize unless he competes according to the rules. The hard-working farmer ought to be the first to receive his share of the crops."

1. "Be strong in the grace that is in Christ Jesus" means to focus on God's grace.
2. "Entrust to faithful men" could mean to enlarge our sphere of influence.
3. "Suffer hardship" refers to doing whatever it takes, be willing to go through hard times.
4. "Be a good soldier" is saying to be disciplined, a team player, focused.
5. "Do not entangle yourself with the affairs of everyday life" is talking about staying focused, know your purpose, don't get distracted from your purpose.
6. "Compete as an athlete" means to play by the rules, visualize "no pain – no gain."
7. "The hard-working farmer ought to be the first to receive his share of the crops" speaks of rewarding yourself, and having personal incentives.

Saying that we need to be centered on God's grace, but also strong in being disciplined and focused, with motivation and purpose can summarize this passage.

You may not agree with everything I pointed out about these passages, but I think you will agree that there is a striking similarity between these verses and what self-help success books teach.

Remember, success can be defined in many ways. The Bible says that God wants His people to be successful. There are specific verses that say that. One example is Joshua 1:8.

"This book of the law shall not depart from your mouth, but you shall meditate on it day and night, so that you may be careful to do according to all that is written in it; for then you will make your way prosperous, and then you will have success."

As I have stated many times already, success is a journey and the destination is not as important as what we become in the process. On our journey God will allow us to go through a lot of hardship and heartache in order to mold our character. If success is just about money and wealth, I would have no business writing this chapter, but I can still be considered a success without these things. Consider the following definitions of success:

1. Success is persistence, refusing to quit.
2. Success is developing one's potential.
3. Success is not settling for less than God's best.

According to these definitions, over the last several years I have been very successful, even though I do not have the income or the material goods to show for it.

God has laid down many principles in His Word because He wants us to do well in life. If we do not follow those principles, He will many times, through His grace, bless us anyway. God knows we mess up. We make poor choices.

Here is a personal example. As I have stated earlier in my story, because of poor choices and mindsets of the past that have resulted in me being so broke, I have almost always driven old cars. A few years ago I had a car that completely quit running, and I had no money to fix it up or buy another one. I was wondering what I was going to do. As I was sitting at my kitchen table talking to God about it, the telephone rang. The voice on the other end said, "John, do you need a car? I have one I will give to you." I nearly dropped the phone out of shock, especially because I had not mentioned a thing to this person about my need for a car. WOW! God's grace is so good!

I would like to share two statements that help me stay focused on my vision and purpose, these two life statements help me to become a better person, and therefore successful, regardless of how little money I have.

1. I am taking advantage of every moment and opportunity to develop my potential for God's glory, and to influence as many people as possible in a positive way.
2. I am helping heal the hurts, habits and hang-ups of people around me through compassion, listening, sharing of myself, patience, unconditional love, and giving.

Of all the success principles I have read, some have taken hold in my life. The ones listed below are those that are working best for me. They help keep me focused with a positive, success-oriented, God-honoring mindset.

1. Stay Focused. Stay focused on God's grace. I try to not allow my problems to become bigger than God. With His grace there are no such words as "can't," "impossible," or "hopeless." I must stay focused on my purpose, vision, dreams, and goals.
2. Have Goals and Vision. I must get out of my rut of daily living and do something with my life that will make a lasting, positive impact in the lives of my family and others. Dream big for God's glory. Have dreams that are God initiated and directed.
3. It Is Never Too Late to Learn and Leap Ahead. I have read story after story of people who have had great dreams and accomplished much with their lives when they were in their 80's and 90's. To say I am too old is a limiting thought. In fact, I can prolong my life by keeping a vision and purpose.
4. Always Work on Self-Improvement. There is nothing unbiblical or unspiritual about bettering myself for more effectively serving God and others. I have a sister-in-law who decided to learn Spanish. As a result she has seen a person come to accept Christ, that she witnessed to in Spanish.

5. Don't Be Held Back by Obstacles. Am I a winner or a whiner? Be a positive thinker who refuses to quit. Find or make a way to accomplish my goals.
6. Do What Makes Me Happy. It is not spiritual to have a "martyr complex." In fact, it might be a result of low self esteem. Do not be controlled by the expectations of others. Be happy in fulfilling my goals and dreams.
7. Always Have Options. Try to get into a position where I do not always have to do things just because I need the money. Follow my heart. Ask myself the question: "What would I really like to do with my life to honor God if I had some choices?" That may require one to become financially independent.
8. Have Mentors. Develop a group of people who are committed to my personal growth, and that I can talk to about anything. Get people who share my vision. Get into a support group, if necessary.
9. Do Something Every Day Toward Improving Yourself or Obtaining Your Goals. This requires passion and purpose.
10. Save Money Regularly. With enough money saved over a long period of time, even small amounts every month, I am less likely to be in financial bondage.
11. Refuse to Worry About Things Over Which I Have No Control. This unnecessarily saps my mental energy and distracts me from my goals and focus. Someone said that worry is like a rocking chair. It gives you something to do, but accomplishes nothing. Turn worry, doubt, and fear into worship and positive affirmations.
12. Be Proactive. Proactively take charge of situations within my control before they become a source of worry and distraction.
13. Expect Good Things to Happen Every Day. Claim God's favor. It says in Psalm 5:12 that we are surrounded with a shield of favor. Believe that any adversity that comes into

our lives will have an equal or greater benefit. God can cause all things to develop our character.

14. Acknowledge God's Sovereignty and Timing. Patience is trusting God's timing. Do not expect life to give me breaks, but God's grace will.
15. Be A Giver. Give to the local church, and other ministries and charities, with my time, talents, and money. Help people in need. I will follow the admonitions of I Corinthians 16:2, II Corinthians 8:2-3 and 9:7. I will cheerfully give what I have purposed in my heart to give.

I will conclude this chapter by giving my own definition of success from a Christian perspective:

Success is persistently moving forward, choosing how I use my time and activities in which to become involved, so that I will make the most of my gifts and abilities, following my heart, and take advantage of every opportunity to have a positive, spiritual impact on as many people as possible, with the goal of seeing changed lives. This may involve getting into a position where I can more and more *choose* what I do with my life, and bound less and less with doing things just because I have to.

I am seeking to make the most of where I am right now in my life. I am pointing toward my potential, which is the subject of the next chapter.

Chapter 10

POINTING TOWARD YOUR POTENTIAL

"I will go anywhere as long as it is forward." David Livingston, Missionary
"What is worse than being blind? Having sight without vision." Helen Keller.

Sometimes the only thing we can change is ourselves. Success is not so much what one is in the best of times, but how a person responds to situations in the worst of times. That is what really reveals one's character. One thing we can always do is continually work at making the most of ourselves. We can "bloom where we are planted."

I could not do any of these things at the low point of my life. I felt like I was not a person of value, or had nothing to give to anyone. No matter what our problems are and how lowly we think of ourselves, God never thinks lowly of us. Romans 8:1 has a word of encouragement. "There is therefore now no condemnation for those who are in Christ Jesus." When it comes to recovery, that is one of the most comforting verses in the Bible. The immediate context of verses 35-39 lists all of the things that are unable to separate us from the love of God: tribulation, distress, persecution, famine, nakedness, peril, sword, death, life, angels, principalities, things present, things to come, powers, height, depth, or any other created thing. I am greatly encouraged to know that my problems do not separate me from God's love.

This brings me to the subject of God's grace. Without an acknowledgement of God's grace, I cannot develop my potential. Because of His grace, I can deal with my past and not allow it to pollute my future. I can get on with my life. All of the things I mentioned previously that I have had to do to recover do not overshadow God's grace.

Because of God's grace I have excellent health that enables me to provide for my family, pursue my interests, and develop my potential. By His grace I go about my daily routine without being involved in a serious accident that could disable me for the rest of my life, but even that could have great potential. Developing our potential all starts with the health and safety within God's protective care. We can have GPS: God's Protective Surveillance.

There is another side to this, however. It is called human effort. That term is taboo among some Christians. The argument is that a Christian should be trusting God and not relying upon his or her own strength. Is that supposed to mean that we are not to do anything ourselves?

I have been exposed to some thinking that leads me to believe that some people think that once you have become a Christian, you should just do away with your brain. Some Christians shy away from thinking that we should recognize our own abilities. Here is what I am getting at. Non-Christians will use any means to get ahead in life without consulting God. Decisions are made based upon intelligence, creativity, and decision-making ability, using the brain with which God created them. Then they become a Christian and hear people telling them to "talk to God" about every little detail of their lives. They are told to always "pray about it," or "see what God would have you do." I am not intending to make light of consulting God and seeking His will, but are we to toss the thinking capacity and abilities with which God has blessed us out the window? There are verses scattered all through Scripture that stress using our own free will to make choices when it comes to being disciplined, persistent, and pressing on.

Here is what I believe to be the balance between "using our brain" and "consulting God." We should make plans, set goals, dream big, and then "go for the gold for God," with everything we have. As we do this we need to recognize that God is in control, that He is sovereign, His timing is perfect, and if for some reason He wants to redirect our life, then we are open to His leading. I will illustrate this point with the following equation:

Good self-esteem Being persistent Setting goals Being positive	+	**Recognizing God's Sovereignty and God's Timing**	=	**God's best opportunities and Reaching God's Goals for your life**

The opposite can be true in a negative sense:

God's best opportunities and His goals and purposes for you	-	**Being negative Being a quitter Having low self- esteem with no goals**	=	**Less than God's best and not obtaining all that He has for you (Living a settle-for life)**

It all boils down to making the most of our lives. Do the very best we can with the resources we have. Stretch ourselves. Get rid of limiting thoughts. Leave our comfort zones. Take steps of faith. Believe God for the ultimate best. Somehow make our lives count for God, and determine to make a positive difference in the lives of others. Make a conscious decision that, by God's grace, no matter what you have been through, it will be used to help heal the hidden hurts of other people. That is another reason why I am writing this book. Wouldn't it be great if Christians put forth as much zeal, effort, and discipline in developing their relationship with God and effectiveness with others, as businessmen put forth in developing a successful business or becoming a millionaire? There is nothing wrong, of course, with simply going to work day after day, to meet the needs of our family, but even that can become a rut. Someone once said a rut can be defined as a "grave with no ends." I encourage you to rise above the rut.

Pray the Prayer of Jabez. This prayer, which is found in I Chronicles 4:9-10, lists four elements. The first one mentioned is asking God to bless his life. Next, Jabez wants God to enlarge his borders. Some people have stated that another way to think of this is that Jabez desires to have a greater sphere of influence. This is expressing a desire to make a greater impact for God, and to enlarge our borders we have to be willing to step out of our comfort zones. Furthermore, he prays for God's hand to be upon him. His final request is that he does not want to be a pain. Jabez stands above everyone else listed in this passage of Scripture. Jabez refused to be in a rut.

As important as it is to wake up in the morning, go to work, be involved in activities and ministries, and then get up the next morning and do this all over again, God wants us to both experience His blessings and to be a blessing to others, along the way. People need to "stop and smell the roses." God desires for us to be "the light of the world" and "the salt of the earth." Rise above the rut and stand out for Christ. We can stand above the crowd by the way we respond to people, situations, and opportunities that God causes to cross our path.

Recently, while on my way to work, I stopped by the local auto parts store. Upon entering the store, I saw a man standing at the counter whom I knew from the recovery ministry at church. When he saw me, he took me outside because he wanted to talk about something that was on his heart. God, through His timing of causing our routines of living to cross paths, presented an opportunity to rise above the rut.

We can rise above the rut by determining to make our lives count. What are some things you can do to make the most of who you are, and where you are at this particular point in your life? I have already mentioned that for me it was writing this book. Follow your heart. I think some Christians have allowed people to tell them it is unspiritual and shows a lack of surrender to follow their hearts and dreams. Do what you want to do and glorify God through it.

H – Hear (and obey) God's Word
E – Strive for Excellence
A – Attitude
R – Reach & Run toward your goal and the course that God has for you
T – Be true to yourself and teach others

What is surrender? It does not mean to never have goals and plans. It is a willingness to give up one's plans. Allow me to use the writing of this book as an example. Suppose, after putting in countless hours of following my dream and passion of preparing this manuscript for publication, God told me to no longer continue because He has a different course for my life. Would I be willing to drop it right then and there?

If we follow our heart, we must keep our heart right with God. It does not matter, however, what other people think. True, we need to be sensitive to what our spouse and family thinks and guard against relationships being destroyed, but we cannot allow other people to hold us back in life.

What abilities do we have? I have heard some Christians say that the best kind of ability is availability. That is true as long as it is not a substitute for what one really ought to be doing. I believe God detests mediocrity. If a person is not careful there can be availability without ability, which can lead to doing something to no avail. There are areas of ministry that require some degree of ability in order to do it right. We cannot let just anyone do it. Music is one such example. God deserves our very best. Why get involved in something in which we know we have little or no ability unless God directs us to do so? It sometimes is a good idea to examine our priorities and involvements, and ask the question, "Is what I am doing making the greatest use of my God-given potential, and having the greatest impact on the greatest number of people.

The local and universal church needs expert, professional people trained in every area. Why should we cut corners with God? Step forward and use your training and education as another step toward maximizing your potential. We should try not to allow any idea, thought, belief, or attitude to stand in the way of moving ahead for God. Satan has many ways of causing us to be negative thinkers and come up with excuses. Are we resting on what we know, or stretching so we will grow?

Another way we can point toward our potential, in addition to using our abilities and training, is to exercise our spiritual gifts. Exercising our spiritual gifts is a way to bear fruit for God and rise above the routine of living. They are given to every believer by the grace of God. Three Scripture passages list them: I Corinthians 12:1-11 & 28-31, Romans 12: 6-8 and Ephesians 4:11. If you are a Christian and unsure of what your spiritual gift or gifts might be, I encourage you to read these verses of Scripture.

There are many things I could say about spiritual gifts, but I would like to point out one insight that pertains to self-esteem. I Corinthians says that everyone is important because of his or her gifts. Believers need not think or say, "I am nobody." One of the reasons for gifts is to maximize one's effectiveness for God. I once heard a college pastor tell me three ways to identify a spiritual gift. One, you will desire it. Two, others will recognize it. Three, God will bless it. There are several spiritual gifts inventories available. Check with your local Christian bookstore or your Christian education director.

Last, but certainly of prime importance, is to associate with the right people. Just because people call themselves Christians and you see them in church every week, does not mean that they are a good influence on you. They may be negative, have a critical spirit, and gossip about others. Be around the kind of people who will help you point toward your potential.

Before I go any further, I would like to review the elements that play a part in propelling our lives in a positive direction.

1. We must remember that we can always take the initiative to bring about changc that is within our control.
2. We can make a decision to simply refuse to think lowly of ourselves because there is no condemnation in Christ.
3. God's grace makes it possible to fulfill our potential by His protective care for our health and safety.
4. We should use the brain with which God created us by making well-informed, wise, and common sense decisions and choices, that are God-honoring and will bring positive results.
5. Do the most with the resources we have and where we are in life. "Do what you can where you can."
6. Pray the prayer of Jabez.
7. Follow our hearts and dreams.
8. Use our abilities, training and education in the local and universal churches.
9. Exercise our spiritual gifts.
10. Associate with the right kind of people.
11. Be available to God and do whatever He wants, regardless of our gifts, dreams, or abilities.
12. Make every effort not to be in financial bondage.

Please allow me to expand on this last point. In my experience, financial bondage, just like worry, doubt, and fear, can block God's thoughts that can thrust us ahead in life and into experiencing His best. Therefore, I need to continually work at removing all "mental clutter" from my mind, if I am trying to forge ahead for God.

Now let's turn our attention to the role that parents have in developing our potential. Consider the possibility that you can stifle your dreams by doing what your parents think you ought to be doing. If you really want to follow in their footsteps, fine, but if you are doing it solely to live up to their expectations, you may be missing out on God's best for your life. Being affirmed by your parents at an early age, regarding what you want to do is extremely important. Lack of affirmation can lead to low self-esteem. Children can interpret this to mean that what they want to do with their lives is not important to the parent. Then children can begin to wonder how much value they have to their parents.

I want to have a goal of becoming all that I can be, and doing all that I can for God's glory. GOAL = GO with you're AL(L). I want to move ahead with big dreams and goals, and do whatever it takes to accomplish those goals. I work on my book almost every day, sometimes getting up early before I leave for work. I cannot focus however, on what I cannot change, if I am going to move ahead. Moving ahead in life means I must allow God to change what I cannot, and to fix what is broken.

Did you hear the joke about how many psychiatrists it takes to change a light bulb. The answer is, only one provided the light bulb wants to change.

Success at developing God's potential for my life is coming as a result of allowing Him to fix what has been broken and to make changes in my life that He knows need to be made to point me to my potential.

An "emotional picture" I like to use is comparing each day with a clean piece of paper. I can do several things with a piece of paper. I can crumble it up, throw it in the trashcan, or totally waste it. I can draw a creative and beautiful picture on it that may brighten up someone's life. I can write down an idea on it that may change the world.

To experience our full potential, however, we must be under the control of the Holy Spirit. That means we must *not* be under the control of any person, thing or circumstance.

Let's take a brief look at how many things can control us if we allow them to:

1. Another person (their expectations or approval, not having boundaries, or being bound by their "shoulds and should nots.")
2. A job or an employer
3. A belief system that is unbiblical, like tradition, or legalism.

4. Our problems
5. Our feelings
6. Our circumstances
7. Low self-esteem, anger, codependency, etc.
8. Money (or lack of)
9. Negative thinking
10. The media and advertising
11. Sports, especially football!
12. Comparison with others

Many others could come to mind if we took the time to brainstorm. God's Holy Spirit can fill our minds with His thoughts that will move us along to experience the potential He has for us, when we deal with the negative strongholds of our thinking that block Him from doing so. Again, we must do whatever is necessary to be "transformed by the renewing of our minds," and "bring every thought captive into the obedience of Christ."

Every day people can choose what to do with their lives. It takes discipline, focus, and a positive attitude. I must expect good things to happen. I must recognize the opportunities that God sends my way. Sometimes there will be setbacks. When there are, or when we fail, we can always look to God's grace and the cross, for the strength to get up and carry on.

Several years ago my family went to Disneyland, and on the way to our hotel, which was on Chapman Avenue, we got completely lost. We remembered the Crystal Cathedral with its huge, tall cross was also located on this street. When we looked to the cross, we found our way to our destination.

If you are not a Christian, I invite and encourage you right now to call upon His grace. It is a historical fact that 2000 years ago, a person named Jesus Christ, who claimed to be fully man and fully God, died on a cross for you. Simply acknowledge that you are a sinner, meaning you are separated from God, and need His forgiveness. Then invite Him into your heart, and allow Him to do whatever He wants to with your life. You will not only have eternal life, but will have added incentive to live to your full potential for His glory. John 3:16 says, "*For God so loved the world, that He gave His only begotten son, that whosoever believes in Him, should not perish, but have everlasting life.*" Then John 10:10 says that Christ "*came that they might have life and might have it abundantly.*"

Developing one's potential all points toward bearing fruit.

Chapter 11

FASHIONED FOR FRUITFULNESS

God wants to work on us from the Inside out.

The subject of this chapter is becoming a fruitful, productive, and victorious Christian. Before that can occur we must be aware of the things in our lives that are hindrances to that happening, and concurrently be taking steps to deal with them. It is a limiting thought to think that the "trash" in our lives is no big deal! Even though God has forgiven us and His grace is transforming us, the garbage in our lives can still get in the way of our relationships with ourselves, others and God. It can hinder our effectiveness in helping other people and serving God, and can slow down the recovery process. I have gotten to the point where I measure my spiritual walk not by religious activities, prayer and Bible reading, but by my degree of indifference to sin in my life.

I continue to learn more and more about God's grace as I deal with my struggles. His grace is not based upon what I do or don't do. It is not based on how hard I work to overcome my struggles. However, I never want to take advantage of His grace by doing *nothing* to change. God, however, does not withhold His grace because I cannot "get my act together."

God continues to reveal insights from His Word that speak about recovery. A few months ago in my Bible reading, I came across a neat sequence of verses. These verses are quite well known, but it is their order that is significant. There are five principles based on these verses.

Principle number one is that we become the kind of person we dwell on. This is mentioned in Proverbs 23:7 which says as a man "thinks within himself so he is."

Principle number two is that we can get rid of incorrect thinking by disciplining our thought life to think like Christ. II Corinthians 10:5, quoted several times already in this book, tells us to take "every thought captive to the obedience of Christ." As I have stated earlier an excellent way to do this is to memorize, personalize, and visualize Scripture.

Principle number three is, we can think differently and therefore, be different. Romans 12:2 states we can be "transformed by the renewing of your mind."

Principle number four is, we will experience God's compassion and pardon when we seek to change our thinking and our ways. This is based on Isaiah 55:7, "Let the wicked forsake his way, and the unrighteous man his thoughts, and let him return to the Lord, and He will have compassion on him; and to our God, for He will abundantly pardon."

Principle number five is, we are powerless, and must rely upon God to bring total change. Romans 7:25 says, "…so then, on the one hand I myself with my mind am serving the law of God, but on the other, with my flesh the law of sin."

In seeing God bring change, we must cooperate with Him. A big part of that involves getting rid of all negative influences in our life. We will not be fruitful and victorious until we do. People can be genuine and sincere believers, but still have one or more of the following negative, destructive influences. We are caught up in a spiritual battle, and these things "add fuel to Satan's fire."

1. Bad childhood programming and experiences that have never been dealt with.
2. Habits and negative, destructive patterns of behavior that have become strongholds in a person's subconscious.
3. Bad Bible teaching and application.
4. Wrong thinking about God, others, and ourselves (for example, an unforgiving spirit.)

5. Association with the wrong groups of people, like negative thinkers or legalistic, judgmental churches.
6. Exposing our eyes and ears to destructive media like some television programs (including news), movies, video games, books, musical lyrics (notice, I said lyrics, not style). I did not say *all* of these things. There is good and bad in all media. We need to be selective in what we watch or listen to.
7. Focusing on the problem, instead of the solution. I have talked about this extensively in this book.
8. Sometimes thinking that a "15-minute quiet time" is all that is needed, when it really requires an all-day application, with hard work, brutal self-honesty, forgiveness, and unconditional love.

Romans 13:14 exhorts the believer to "Put on the Lord Jesus Christ, and *make no provision for the flesh in regard to its lusts*."

That is why I have what I refer to as a "spiritual arsenal," consisting of books, memory verses, Christian TV programs, small support groups, mentors, and Bible reading. I also use the power of words to combat Satan and keep me focused.

In everything we do all day long, every day, we must strive to be consistent with what the Bible teaches. We must saturate our minds with spiritual truth and influences. But no matter how much discipline and obedience we have, we all fall short. Romans 3:23 says, "For all have sinned, and fall short of the glory of God." However, be careful and do not make the mistake that I made most of my life, thinking that God is going to bring about change in my life without my working at it.

Does the grace of God and our discipline work together? They most certainly do, according to I Corinthians 15:10. "But by the grace of God I am what I am, and His grace toward me did not prove vain, but I labored even more than all of them, yet not I, but the grace of God with me."

The bottom line is, do we through discipline and God's grace, have mastery over our problems, or do our problems master us?

When our problems control us, we have loss of self-esteem. We may begin to lose hope. We feel trapped and are living in bondage. Sometimes we feel like I did, guilty and condemned. It does not have to be this way. I have just mentioned many of the things that get in the way of having victory. Now, let us turn our attention to God's power that gives us the *desire and discipline* to see change.

Romans, chapters 6-8, has many verses that speak to this issue:

6:1-2 – "What shall we say then? Are we to continue in sin that grace might increase? May it never be!..."

6:6 – "Knowing this, that our old self was crucified with Him, that our body of sin might be done away with, that we should no longer be slaves to sin." (II Peter 2:19 reinforces this teaching: "... By what a man is overcome, by this he is enslaved.")

6:12 – "Therefore do not let sin reign in your mortal body that you should obey its lusts."

6:13 – "And do not go on presenting the members of your body to sin as instruments of unrighteousness..."

6:15 – "What then? Shall we sin because we are not under law but under grace? May it never be!"

6:18 – "And having been freed from sin, you became slaves of righteousness."

All of these verses emphasize being liberated from sin, and notice how stress is placed upon conscious choice and determination. But even our choices are tainted by our sin nature. Romans 7:15-21 says,

"*For that which I am doing, I do not understand; for I am not practicing what I would like to do, but I am doing the very thing I hate. But if I do the very thing I do not wish to do, I agree with the Law, confessing that it is good. So now, no longer am I the one doing it, but sin which indwells me. For I know that nothing good dwells in me, that is, in my flesh; for the wishing is present in me, but the doing of the good is not. For the good that I wish, I do not do; but I practice the very evil that I do not wish. But if I am doing the very thing I do not wish, I am no longer the one doing it, but sin which dwells in me. I find then the principle that evil is present in me, the one who wishes to do good.*"

The Word of God has so much insight. There are several important principles seen in these verses. The first one, which we have already discussed many times before, is that what we practice we become. Let's stop and talk about that word "practice." As a musician when I practice, I discipline myself to do something over and over again, until it becomes so engrained in me that I can do it without thinking about it. My instrument becomes an extension of me. The opposite is also true. If we practice things that are not consistent with the Bible, we will not have victory. Two, *wishing* never accomplishes anything. Three, we are powerless to have victory by our own discipline.

Verses 23-25 talk about the battle of the mind. How we think, and what we dwell on all starts in the mind. I heard a story long ago about a man who had two dogs. One dog was named Flesh. The other was named Spirit. These two dogs were always getting into fights. Someone asked the man, "Which dog usually wins?" The man responded by saying, "Whichever one I feed the most."

Chapter 8 begins by saying, "There is therefore now no condemnation for those who are in Christ Jesus," and it ends by telling us, "But in all these things we overwhelmingly conquer through Him who loved us. For I am convinced that neither death, nor life, nor angels, nor principalities, nor things present, nor things to come, nor powers, nor height, nor depth, nor any other created thing, shall be able to separate us from the love of God, which is in Christ Jesus our Lord." (37-39)

Notice this verse says, "For those who are in Christ Jesus." If you are not a Christian and have destructive practices, your struggle is more difficult because you have no diving power to back you up. You have no forgiveness. You need to surrender to Him, but it will still require effort. A flower grows through dirt. God uses the grit and grime in our lives to help us grow through His grace.

Can God use you the way you are? That is a question I have asked myself many times during my recovery. It has much to do with having hope. You may have gone through divorce, used drugs, had an addiction to gambling, or had a problem with anger and low self-esteem. However, if you have now committed your life to Christ, it is not too soon to seek God for how He wants to use you. Remember, your greatest hurt can become your greatest ministry. You might say one thing to someone that will help him.

It is very interesting to me that right in the middle of the Romans 6-8 passage is a verse that emphasizes bearing fruit. "Therefore, my brethren, you also were made to die to the Law through the body of Christ, that you might be joined to another, to Him who was raised from the dead, that we might bear fruit for God." (7:4) In the midst of our struggles, God does not necessarily put us in the wilderness. God's ultimate purpose for us is to bear fruit. Read Galatians 5:22-23, Hebrews 12:11, Luke 3:8, Matthew 7:16-20, Matthew 13:23, John 15:1-5, Colossians 1:10, Psalm 1, and Hebrews 13:15. These are only several out of a multitude scattered throughout the Bible.

God wants to bless our lives, but not always in the way that some people think, with money and wealth. He desires for us to have a sphere of influence where we can make a difference, and experience His power and presence. We can bear the fruit of the Spirit, the fruit of souls won to the Lord, and the fruit of an abundant life.

Consider some individuals from the Bible. Moses was a murderer, but God used him to deliver the children of Israel. The Apostle Paul was a persecutor of Christians until he became one himself. Peter denied Christ three times, but later went on to be a pillar of faith for Christ. I could go on and on. God did not use these people based on their past. God does not hold grudges against you.

God can give you a new beginning. He can heal your hurts and can use you to help the hurts of others. Believe in yourself and believe in God's power and plan for your life. Hopefully, God has used this book as a tool to help send you on your way to recovery.

God is anxiously waiting to help you fulfill your potential and purpose.

You may be wondering how to begin to fulfill and experience God's best?

1. Start by reading the Bible. God's will is spelled out very specifically in the pages of the inspired Word. It will tell you the kind of person God wants you to become. Pay particular attention to the verses that deal with developing character qualities and doing His will. Romans 15:4 states, "For whatever was written in earlier times was written for our instruction, that through perseverance and the encouragement of the Scriptures we might have hope."
2. Next, get connected to Christians and a local church that will support you in your recovery. This can include mentoring, small groups, and if you can afford one, a counselor. Some large churches have counselors on their staff.
3. Determine that you are going to make your life count for something through becoming all that you can become, and by having a positive impact on the lives of others, starting with your own family.
4. Make a decision that by your attitude, example, and how you respond to situations, you are not going to allow what you cannot change, to keep you from changing what you can.
5. Take advantage of every opportunity, even in the worst of times, and with whatever limitations you may have, to bear fruit for God.

This diagram shows many of the things we can do to use our potential for God's glory. Everything we do, however, is foundational upon God's grace and sovereignty. It all points toward bearing fruit.

Pointing Toward Your Potential

Reading **Change What You Can** **Claim God's Favor** **Be A Positive Thinker** **Determine to Make Your Life Count** **Pray the Prayer of Jabez** **Get Out of Your "Rut"** **Deal With The Obstacles**	**Bear Fruit** **God's Grace** **The Cross** **No Condemnation** **God's Protective Care** **His Sovereignty and Timing**	**Prayer/Bible Study** **Scripture Memory** **Associate With the Right People** **Expect Good Things to Happen** **Utilize Your Spiritual Gifts** **Use Your Abilities and Professional Training** **Do the Best With What You Have** **Follow Your Dreams** **Dream Big**

To develop my potential and bear fruit, I have discovered that I must set things in motion that will result in that happening. If God provides an opportunity you have to start working towards it. In my case, it didn't occur just because I was surrendered to God. Being committed to Christ and to His Lordship does not mean I have to give up being success-oriented. It does not mean I cannot follow my dream and goals. Furthermore, I need not do away with my abilities and talents. I should be willing to give up any part of myself to God, but at the same time, be committed to using all that I am and have for God.

The Bible says, "*The truth shall make you free.*" John 8:32. We are made free by knowing ourselves. We are set free by understanding the Word of God as properly interpreted and obeyed. Freedom comes by realizing that we are in a spiritual battle, and Satan will get the upper hand if allowed to. That is why we must "Put on the whole armor of God, and do everything to stand firm." That starts in our mind. Our thinking must be transformed. We must, as I have stated several times already, think correctly about God, ourselves, and others.

That is why I am living a disciplined life of feeding my mind with a constant diet of spiritual truth and positive thoughts that will help me *grow* as an individual and *go* ahead in life. Of course, I have times of fun, relaxation, and entertainment, and I make time to take care of my needs.

If we want to see change take place, we must change the way we use our time. I used to use my time to no purpose, like watching a lot of negative TV, or going to church activities just because it was the expected and accepted thing to do. I have found that it is necessary to *replace* negative, destructive habits and activities, or things that are not moving me ahead in life or helping me grow spiritually, with positive habits and activities that serve a purpose and help me grow.

Now a typical weekly/monthly routine consists of reading the Bible more, memorizing Scripture, reading, working on this book, and watching Christian TV. I am involved in small fellowship groups. I am inviting people out to church and boldly speaking out for God, something I have never before done. I am doing things that make a difference in people's lives. In short, I am becoming the type of Christian I have always felt I needed to be, but wondered why I wasn't.

I got to this point in my life, not because other Christians said I should, but because I saw the need for it. I must keep Satan off my back, so I can experience victory. All of what I have mentioned in the preceding paragraph, and some of what I have discussed in this book, has started to become a positive stronghold, and it is more and more exterminating the negative mindset of the past 50 years! Praise God. I want to emphasize, however, that nothing should take the place of Bible reading and prayer.

I want to make something very clear. I am not yet "practicing all that I preach." I still have many struggles, some limiting thoughts, and negative circumstances that are "stuck" — they are not changing. However, for the first time in my life, I am allowing

God to move me in a positive direction. This book is the culmination of six years of recovery! My recovery will, however, continue long after this book is written and published. God is continually changing my life for the better, and to be more effective for Him.

As a result of being disciplined, I want to get rid of all worry, doubt, and fear. I want to be a blessing to others, and have an attitude of confidently expecting good things to happen. I am choosing to live every day in victory. When I am disciplined, victory is the result. When I am not, I fall.

Through God's grace and power you too can experience God's Healing Hope and break the negative strongholds of your thinking. You can become a prisoner of hope through the positive strongholds that God offers, and I believe it starts with transformed thinking.

Many verses in Psalms make reference to God as our stronghold. One in particular is Psalm 9:9. "*The Lord also will be a stronghold for the oppressed, a stronghold in times of trouble.*" The Word of God will transform our lives, and transformation will lead to fruitfulness.

Life's greatest heartbreak, apart from not knowing Christ, is for people to go through their entire existence with no victory over their hurts and struggles. Don't allow yourself to take your past to your grave.

The greatest tragedy for a Christian is to never experience life as God intended and to never have a positive, spiritual influence on the life of another person.

Hopefully, through the reading of this book, you have gained more awareness of how much wrong thinking due to childhood and religious upbringing can impact your present. I have tried to shed some more light on how important self-esteem is in being successful and experiencing God's best. I hope you have come away with a greater recognition of the importance of dealing with the problems and issues of life. It is my prayer that you will see, no matter what it is you are going through, that it is never too late to see change take place.

The only thing that really matters in life can be summed up in two words: changed lives. After we are gone, are you and I going to leave some behind?

Chapter 12

AVOIDING PITFALLS, FOR TEENS AND YOUNG ADULTS

This chapter consists of 13 points of review from this book. However, I have entitled it "Tips for Teens" because each one of these items can have specific application for giving guidance to high school students as they enter the "real world." These are guidelines that parents can discuss and evaluate with their teens before they go out on their own. By doing so, the children may avoid many of the pitfalls that lead to having negative strongholds in their lives, and the hurts and struggles that go along with them.

1. Gauge your self-esteem very early in life. Ask yourself some questions: How did I feel about myself in high school? Have I allowed people to use or abuse me in any way, from as far back as I can remember? Have I just accepted things the way they are? Have I remained silent about things I did not like, or when people did not respect me?
2. Realize how significant your childhood and religious upbringing has been in forming mindsets that can be carried into your adult life. Try to recall specific things that have been said to you, or things that have happened that have had a negative emotional impact. What are some things that you continually dwell on and cannot let go of?
3. Get rid of any emotional baggage from your childhood or family life as soon as possible. It *will* negatively impact you later in life. Be particularly careful not to carry it into

your marriage. Love will not automatically take care of all your problems and heal all of your wounds.

4. Follow your dream, but be obedient to the Word of God.
5. Always believe that change is possible. You do not have to become "stuck" in a mindset or circumstance.
6. You can choose to live a life of victory.
7. Have a clearly defined definition of success from a Christian perspective, and be success-oriented early in life.
8. Always work on self-improvement. Become the best "you" that you can be for God's glory and to more effectively minister to others.
9. Develop your potential. Maximize yourself for God and others by getting out of your comfort zone, using your abilities and spiritual gifts, rising above the rut of living, and "going for the gold for God."
10. Don't get into a credit/spend mindset. Save money regularly. Don't allow yourself, to the best of your control, to get into financial bondage. Financial bondage can be a major distraction and hindrance from doing what you really want to do with your life, and can keep you from being focused on what really matters. Example: Most people would probably be more prone to thinking about how they are going to pay their bills than winning and discipling others for Christ.
11. Constantly fill your mind, all day long, every day, with positive thoughts and spiritual truth. Get rid of *all* negative influences. Make a commitment to associate only with positive-minded people, expose your mind only to media that has a wholesome message, attend events that have a positive environment, and get involved in a local church that has an uplifting atmosphere and will help you grow.
12. Have a biblical view of God's will. Concentrate on doing what the Bible says believers should do. So much time can be spent trying to discern God's will (even to the point of not moving ahead in life.)

13. Make God, Lord of all. Recognize His sovereignty and timing in all that you do. Focus on God's grace with an attitude of gratitude. He can cause your path to cross with the right people and opportunities, with the right resources, to accomplish His objectives for your life. Claim His favor upon all that you do.

EPILOGUE

A great deal of time has elapsed between the writing and publishing of this manuscript. By the time you are reading this, I will have traveled further down the road of recovery. God will have shown me fresh insights from His Word, provided me with new opportunities for growth, and revealed to me new ways of dealing with my problems. God loves me so much!

Everyone who has read this book is at a different stage in life. No matter where we are, you and I will encounter speed bumps, we will have to take detours at times, and we will be subjected to distractions along the way. May we just keep moving forward, making use of every available resource, and enjoying God's grace. If you have received Christ as your personal Lord and Savior, I will meet you at the end of your own personal journey, when we gather around the throne of God in heaven. We will have an eternity to share with one another. What a blessed hope we have! Have a nice trip.

Hopefully, you have found something in this book that will prove to be helpful to you. If this is the case, or you have requests or comments of any nature, I encourage you to write to me at Healing Hope, P.O. Box 616 Zillah, Washington, 98953, USA. You can order books by calling 1-888-232-4444.

Appendix I

BIBLE VERSES ON RECOVERY

Joshua 3:5

Psalms: There are many verses scattered throughout this book. Read the entire book.

Proverbs 28:13

Isaiah 25:4; 30:18; 33:2,6; 40:29-31; 41:10, 17-18; 42:6, 9; 43:18-19; 45:1-2; 49:16; 55:6-9; 57:15,18; 58:6-12; 59:1: 60:1; 61:1

Jeremiah 8:18; 10:23-24; 16:19-21; 29:11-13; 31:2-3, 17, 21; 32:17,27; 33:3; 42:6

Matthew 11:28-30; 26:41

Mark 8:33; 9:23

Luke 9:23

John 11:40

Acts 3:19, 7:10

Romans 8:37

I Corinthians 3:16; 6:19-20; 10:12-14; 16:13-14

II Corinthians 2:14, 7:1

Galatians 1:24; 2:20; 5:1, 16, 22-26

Ephesians 3:12, 20; 6:10-11, 13

Hebrews 4:16; 10:23

I Peter 1:13; 3:8-9

I John 4:4

Appendix 2

STUDY GUIDE QUESTIONS FOR SMALL GROUPS OR SUNDAY SCHOOL

1. Have you come to recognize, as a result of reading this book, certain things in your life that need to be dealt with?
2. Are there any recognizable mindsets or attitudes that could be holding you back or limiting God from moving you forward in life, or doing what He desires to do in and through your life?
3. How did you answer the "How About You?" sections in chapters 1-5?
4. What are your abilities, interests, and spiritual gifts?
5. Are there any Scripture passages that you do not understand, that could be keeping you from growing in your relationship with God, other people, and yourself?
6. Are there issues in your life that are keeping you from forming and maintaining positive relationships.
7. Of all the recovery "methods" mentioned in chapter 8, which ones do you believe could be of most help to you? Why?
8. Go back over the "Self-test" at the end of chapter 5. Discuss those in which you feel you need to have an "attitude adjustment?"
9. Do you shy away from success books and, if so, why?

10. Choose 1 of the success books listed in the bibliography, check it out from the library, and list as many things as possible, as you read through it, that line up with Scripture.
11. Of the 15 success principles given in chapter 9, which ones do you think could be most useful for you to apply to your life?
12. How would you rate your local church regarding its attitude toward people in need of recovery and healing? Circle the words or phrases that apply, and then have a discussion. Judgmental, accepting, legalistic, offering hope, a haven for healing, welcoming with open arms, cold, turning away, compassionate.
13. Discuss the equations given in chapter 10 on page 108.
14. Review the 12 elements listed on page 112 of chapter 10, that have to do with propelling our lives in a positive direction. Which ones do you believe would help you the most? Review the controlling influences on pages 113-114 of the same chapter. Which ones control you the most?
15. Of the 8 "destructive influences" listed in chapter 11, which ones do you see as necessary to eliminate from your life?
16. Discuss the diagram "Pointing Toward your Potential," in chapter 11, on page 123.
17. Write out your typical week/month. (activities, church events, how you use your time). How much of that is causing you to grow, is having an impact in the lives of other people, and fulfilling God's purpose for you?
18. What are some positive ways you can replace how you use your time, and will allow God to mold you into a fruitful Christian?
19. What would *you like to do* as a Christian, to make your life have a significant impact for God's glory?
20. Have you started to ponder what God's dream and vision is for you? What do you believe is your passion? How would you define the word "passion?"

Author Bio

John Clark grew up in San Diego, California, where he attended San Diego State University. He earned a Bachelor of Arts Degree in music education in 1971, and a teaching certificate in 1973.

He later moved to Portland, Oregon to attend Western Baptist Seminary. In 1979 he graduated with a Master's Degree in Church Music. To fulfill the requirement for his degree, he wrote a thesis entitled, *A Church Music Training and Resource Manual for Laymen*, which is available on microfiche in the libraries of some academic institutions across the United States.

John spent 25 years working in the music field, which mostly included private teaching in voice and trumpet, school teaching, and ministering in churches on the west coast.

Presently John resides in the Yakima Valley of central Washington State, with his wife and son. He was on staff at a church in that area for 10 years. He is now a substitute teacher in three school districts. He is active in a local church and plays in a brass quartet.

TOPICAL RECOMMENDED READING LIST

Attitudes

Rick Foster. *How We Choose to be Happy: The 9 Choices of Extremely Happy People: Their Secrets, Their Stories*. New York: G.P. Putnam's Sons, 1999

Keith Harrell. *Attitude Is Everything: 10 Life-Changing Steps to Turning Attitude Into Action*. New York: Cliff Street Books, 2000

Joel Osteen. *Your Best Life Now: 7 Steps to Living At Your Full Potential*. New York: Warner Faith, 2004

M.J. Ryan. *The Happiness Makeover: How to Teach Yourself to be Happy and Enjoy Everyday Life*. New York: Broadway Books, 2005

Robert H. Schuller. *Move Ahead With Possibility Thinking*. Old Tappan, New Jersey: Fleming H. Revell, 1967

Counseling

Susan Faludi. *Stiffed: The Betrayal of the American Male*. New York: William Morrow, 1999

J. Herzog. *Father Hunger*. Hillsdale, New Jersey: Analytic Press, 2002

Ann Hulbert. *Raising America: Experts, Parents, and a Century of Advice About Children*. New York: Knopf, 2003

Healing

Melody Beattie. *Beyond Codependency And Getting Better All the Time*. Center City, MN: Hazeldon Foundation, 1989.

_____. *Choices: Taking Control of Your Life and Making it Matter*. San Francisco: Harper Publishers, 2002

_____. *Codependent No More: How to Stop Controlling Others and Start Caring For Yourself*. Center City, MN: Hazeldon Foundation, 1992

Cloud. *Boundaries: When to Say Yes, When to Say No, To Take Control of Your Life*. Grand Rapids: Zondervan, 1992

Libby Gil. *Traveling Hopefully: How To Loose Your Family Baggage and Jump Start Your Life*. New York: St. Martin's Press, 2004

Ruth Graham. *In Every Pew Sits A Broken Heart; Hope for the Hurting*. Grand Rapids: Zondervan, 2004

Naomi Judd. *Naomi's Breakthrough Guide: 20 Choices to Transform Your Life*. New York: Simon and Schuster, 2004

Wynonna Judd. *Coming Home to Myself*. New York: New American Library, 2005

Tim LaHaye. *How To Win Over Depression*. Grand Rapids: Zondervan, 1974

Max Lucado. *The Next Door Savior.* Nashville: W. Publishing Group, 2003

Frank Minirth, M.D. *Happiness Is A Choice.* Grand Rapids: Baker Book House, 1978

Robert H. Schuller. *Turn Your Hurts Into Halos.* Nashville: Thomas Nelson, 1999

Charles Swindoll. *Hope Again.* Nashville: Word Publishing, 1996

_____. *Start Where You Are.* Nashville: Word Publishing, 1999

Francine Ward. *Esteemable Acts. 10 Actions for Building Real Self-Esteem.* New York: Broadway Books, 2003

Warren. *Make Anger Your Ally.* Brentwood, TN: Wolgemuth & Hyatt, Publishers, 1990

Tina Zahn. *Why I Jumped: My True Story of Postpartum Depression, Dramatic Rescue & Return to Hope.* Grand Rapids: Fleming H. Revell, 2006

Spiritual Growth

Ann Kiemel Anderson. *This Is A True Story About God: The True Account of Two Men, An Impossible Surgery, and the God of the Universe.* Kansas City: Beacon Hill Press, 1998

Joan Wester Anderson. *Where Miracles Happen: True Stories of Heavenly Encounters.* New York. Brett Books, 1994

Neil Anderson. *Victory Over the Darkness.* Ventura, CA: Regal Books, 1990

Oswald Chambers. *My Utmost For His Highest.* Grand Rapids: Discovery House Publishers, 1992

Larry Christenson. *The Renewed Mind.* Minneapolis: Bethany Fellowship, 1974

James Dobson. *When God Doesn't Make Sense.* Wheaton, Illinois: Tyndale House Publishers, 1993

Jan Dravecky. *A Joy I'd Never Known.* Grand Rapids: Zondervan, 1996

Garry Friesen. *Decision Making and The Will of God: A Biblical Alternative to the Traditional View.* Sisters, Oregon: Multnomah Press, 1980

Billy Graham. *The Journey. How To Live by Faith in an Uncertain World.* Nashville: W. Publishing Group (A division of Thomas Nelson), 2006

Marilyn Hickey. *Break the Generation Curse.* Denver: Marilyn Hickey Ministries, 1988

T.D. Jakes. *Mama Made the Difference: Life lessons My Mother Taught Me.* New York: The Penguin Group, 2006

Grace Ketterman. *You Can Win Over Worry.* Old Tappan, New Jersey: Fleming H. Revell, 1984

Max Lucado. *Cure for the Common Life: Living In Your Sweet Spot.* Nashville: W. Publishing Group, 2005

Joyce Meyer. *Approval Addiction: Overcoming Your Need to Please Everyone*. New York: Time Warner Book Group, 2005

Robert A. Schuller. *Getting Through What You Are Going Through*. Nashville: Thomas Nelson, 1986

Charles Stanley. *How to Handle Adversity*. Nashville: Oliver-Nelson Books, 1989

_____. *When the Enemy Strikes: The Keys to Winning Your Spiritual Battles*. Nashville: Thomas Nelson, 2004

Joni Eareckson Tada. *Ordinary People, Extraordinary Faith*. Nashville: Thomas Nelson, 2001

Rick Warren. *The Purpose Driven Life*. Grand Rapids: Zondervan, 2002

Bruce Wilkinson. *The Prayer of Jabez: Breaking Through to the Blessed Life*. Sisters, Oregon: Multnomah Press, 2000

_____. *Secrets of the Vine*. Sisters, Oregon: Multnomah Press, 2002

Success

Steve Brown. *Overcoming Setbacks*. Colorado Springs: Navpress, 1992

Rob Buess. *Favor: The Road to Success*. Tyler, Texas: Sweeter Than Honey Ministries, 1975

Jack Canfield. *The Success Principles: How to Get From Where You Are to Where You Want to Be*. San Francisco: Harper Collins, 2005

William H. Cook. *Success, Motivation, and The Scriptures.* Nashville: Broadman Press, 1974

Roger Crawford. *How High Can You Bounce? Turn Your Setbacks Into Comebacks.* Bantam Books, 1998

Farrah Gray. *Reallionaire: Nine Steps to Becoming Rich from the Inside Out.* Health Communications, 2004

Spenser Johnson. *Who Moved My Cheese.* New York: G.P. Putnam & Son, 2000

Naomi Judd. *The Transparent Life: 30 Proven Ways to Live Your Best.* Nashville: J. Countryman, A Division of Thomas Nelson, 2005

John Maxwell. *Failing Forward.* Nashville: Thomas Nelson, 2000

Michael J. Ritt. *Napoleon Hill's Key's to Positive Thinking: 10 Steps to Health, Wealth, and Success.* New York: Dutton, 1998

Duke Robinson. *Good Intentions: The Nine Unconscious Mistakes of Nice People.* New York: Warner Books, 1997

Robert H. Schuller. *Don't Throw Away Tomorrow.* San Francisco: Harper Collins, 2005

_____. *My Journey: From An Iowa Farm to a Cathedral of Dreams.* San Francisco: Harper Collins, 2001

_____. *Tough Minded Faith for Tender Hearted People.* Gaston: G.K. Hall, 1985

Hal Urban. *Life's Greatest Lessons: 20 Things That Matter*. New York: Simon and Schuster, 2003

Steve Young. *Great Failures of the Extremely Successful*. Los Angeles: Tall Fellows Press, 2002

www.ingramcontent.com/pod-product-compliance
Ingram Content Group UK Ltd.
Pitfield, Milton Keynes, MK11 3LW, UK
UKHW040602210726
13854UKWH00008B/1712

9 781425 171216